TEN STEPS TO
SUCCESSFUL
PUBLIC SPEAKING

Y

Lothian
BOOKS

To Peter, Jo, Neil and Tania – for your love and support

Thomas C. Lothian Pty Ltd
132 Albert Road, South Melbourne, 3205
www.lothian.com.au

National Library of Australia
Cataloguing-in-Publication data:

Atkins, Mary.
  Finding your voice : ten steps to successful public speaking.

  ISBN 0 7344 0667 3.

  1. Public speaking - Handbooks, manuals, etc. 2. Oral
  communication - Handbooks, manuals, etc. I. Title.

808.51

Cover and text design by Mason Design
Typeset in 10.5/15 pt in Sabon
Printed in Australia by Griffin Press

CONTENTS

ACKNOWLEDGEMENTS

I am most grateful to Toni Childs, Sharon Fricke, Patricia Howard, Peter Howard, Deborah Hutton, Simon Marnie, Lyndey Milan, Tania Nash, Ian Ross and Adam Spencer, who make up the panel of professionals and well-known celebrities who have contributed so generously to this book. A special thanks goes to Marlene Vaughan for supplying the information and advice about correct breathing in Step 8, Voice Matters.

I am grateful to friends and colleagues – Neroli Nelsen from Northern Beaches Communicators, Ian Hamilton from Flying Pig Productions, Stephanie Champion from Champion web Solutions and Charmaine Burke from English Software – for their guidance and review of the text.

In 2003, I rejoined a local speaking club, Northern Beaches Communicators so that I could put my written words to the test and receive valuable feedback from speakers with different levels of experience and expertise. Some of the members are old friends who, over the years, have taught me with gentle and caring evaluation to shape my achievements in my speaking career. I am eternally grateful to them, as well as appreciating the support and encouragement I have received from new members in this project. I would also like to acknowledge the members of my former speaking clubs – Mackellar Communicators and Crows Nest Communicators – who are equally responsible for my growth as a speaker.

It has been said that behind every man is a woman keeping him on track. In my case, my husband Peter has been utterly supportive, always believing completely in me and encouraging me every step of the way, whether in setting up my own company or in writing this book. My family, Jo, Neil and Tania and their partners and children, have also been instrumental in gently pushing me towards achieving my goal of writing this book. All the family are good public speakers, having been influenced by my interest in public speaking, and needless to say I have encouraged them every step of the way to the podium. As you can imagine I am very proud of all of them.

PREFACE

My speaking career was first kindled as an 'air hostess' (the term in those days) when I had to master the 'Welcome on board and please watch the safety instructions' speech over the intercom. Too many years passed before I spoke in public again and, on the first two occasions that I did, I made a complete botch of the job. But speaking from a public platform captured my dreams and I decided I needed some help to achieve this. I joined an international speaking club, where I was a member for over seventeen years. The club's program gave me the confidence and qualifications to communicate well. During this time I won four public-speaking competitions and became an Accredited Trainer in Communication.

In my next role as a national marketer and trainer with an international company, I had to train hundreds of salespeople. After a 'mid-life crisis' change in direction, I became a home economist and started my own company. For nearly two decades my company has provided marketing and event management services to the food and wine industries. During this time I have coached many home economists, chefs and others in public speaking and have enjoyed seeing so many of them achieve recognition in their chosen careers. I have also conceived, produced and presented for TAFE a specifically designed twelve-week Communication/Media Course for students of Food Studies.

I have learned a great deal about the good, bad and undesirable aspects of public speaking from participating on both sides of the podium as a speaker and as an event and conference organiser. My work has led me into broadening my skills with extensive experience in television presentations, live shows and radio broadcasts. I have lectured throughout Australia on food marketing for a national shopping centre group, as well as provided workshops on food service and safety for a major retailing group. I am a past president of the Food Media Club of Australia whose membership is drawn from representatives of the food industry as well as the media. The club's mission statement is 'to communicate food issues and to encourage excellence and professionalism through an exchange of ideas and information'. For the past six years I have been Chair of judges of the Vittoria Australian Food Media Awards. These awards honour outstanding communicators in the media, publishing and food industries.

Having spent more than half my working life training people in a variety of skills, from sales through to cooking techniques, and teaching public-speaking skills, it has been a natural progression to write it all down. As you will see in *Finding Your Voice*, I am passionate about the benefits of learning to speak out in public. I wholeheartedly believe that if you can overcome any fears you might have and use your authentic voice to connect with an audience, it will prove a giant leap forward in your self-development. Seeing people grow in confidence and self-esteem as they master the skills of presenting in public has given me great rewards.

INTRODUCTION

One of life's great challenges is conquering fear. For many people, public speaking is their number one fear, next to dying. For me, my second-greatest fear was writing a book about public speaking. I use the past tense because you know what they say about a 'fear faced' and 'action cures fear'.

Finding Your Voice is a book that can be used by anyone, from an amateur speaker facing a special occasion to the professional presenter. If you are brand new to speaking in public, this book will help you overcome your reservations as you learn how to craft and deliver a speech with self-belief. For speakers who have already been 'blooded', you will find some good reading in revisiting advice and suggestions that you may know, but about which you may have become a little blasé. The information and knowledge in the book will be useful to any speaker, at any stage of their speaking career.

Philosophically, the most important message I can give you in public speaking is to be true to yourself. Be aware of this as you read through each chapter. Anyone can learn to stand up and speak, and do so competently. But when a speaker manages to connect, using words and posture that come from their very being, they really communicate with their audience.

When a speaker masters the fear of being him- or herself, that is when real self-development begins. Too often we allow the mantle of others' opinions to define us. Finding your authentic voice is challenging, but if you adopt the habit of seeking your own truth as you prepare for any public-speaking activity, you will soon be able to overcome any self-limiting beliefs.

Part 1 of *Finding Your Voice* gives you ten easy, confidence-building steps to becoming a successful speaker. These steps provide you with information on how to develop your speech, how to research any necessary resources, and then present it with style and poise. It also incorporates other information that is vital to achieving this success. This includes breathing techniques for better voice production, as well as advice on the care of the voice. You will also find practical information about how to use audiovisual equipment. There is material designed to help you understand and manage stage fright, and a chapter that illustrates the polish and shine of assuming a professional approach to public speaking.

Part 2 looks at a range of speaking assignments where public-speaking skills are in demand. These include occasions such as delivering a eulogy, giving an expression of thanks or a speech of acceptance, acting as master of ceremonies or emcee, interviewing someone, acting as chairperson of a meeting, presenting a workshop or conference speech, being a member of a panel of speakers, taking part in a debate, giving an after-dinner or humorous speech, managing media interviews and giving a demonstration.

Used together, these two parts of *Finding Your Voice* give you the knowledge and guidelines you need to achieve success every time, no matter what the speaking engagement. Each chapter makes use of the elements that you would use in writing a speech: there is a liberal use of quotations, some anecdotal stories, and, at the core, basic information to guide and build your knowledge of speaking in public.

A series of hints and advice, called Celebrity Tips, gives you the opportunity to gain from the experiences of people who make their living from public speaking. These contributors come from different backgrounds, including a strong contingent from the electronic media. Their thoughts, comments, ideas and advice, learned from hard-won experience, will give you valuable pointers to help you achieve successful outcomes in your public speaking.

While a speaker cannot be 'all things to all people', the more prepared you are for all eventualities, the better chance you have of gaining appreciation and approval from the majority of your audience. When you get all the elements of speech-making right and you sincerely connect with your audience, you receive immense personal gratification. I hope this book is instrumental in giving you the tools to hone your speaking skills and that when you 'find your voice' and stand to speak, you too will experience the buzz you get from communicating well with your audience.

CONTRIBUTORS

Toni Childs is an American singer and songwriter, a 2004 Emmy award-winner, who describes her voice 'as being that of an eighty-year-old black woman'. She is well known in Australia for the song 'Many Rivers to Cross' which featured in the National Bank advertising campaign. She works tirelessly for ending violence against women and recently starred in the Hawaiian production of the *Vagina Monologues*.

Shannon Fricke is passionate about renovating and interior design, which shines through in her role as on-air stylist for The LifeStyle Channel's series *Home*. She started her career in magazine publishing. She has been beauty editor, style editor and general editor on magazines ranging from *CLEO* to *Australian Good Taste*.

Patricia Howard, after a long career in the Paul Getty Museum in California, has established herself as a well-loved and respected teacher of yoga. She has presented yoga for children on television in North America and recently overcame her fear of presenting to a large audience by appearing in the Hawaiian production of the *Vagina Monologues*.

Peter Howard has had over fourteen years in television as the food editor of the Nine Network's *Today Show*. He is a food and wine commentator, the author of fifteen books and is food editor for *Friday Magazine*, Rural Press. Peter is a popular presenter on the speaking and show circuit. He is also a councillor of the Royal Agricultural Society of New South Wales.

Deborah Hutton started her working career at the age of sixteen as a model and since then has become one of the most recognisable and best-known personalities of modern Australia. She is editor-at-large of *The Australian Women's Weekly*, as well as being the host of a number of top-rating Nine Network shows. She is also an ambassador for Qantas, Holden, and Medallist, and amongst other things acts as host at their major events. Deborah's style and grace make her an in-demand host for prestigious events such as the Christopher Reeve/Spinal Research Centre fundraising dinner with an audience of 2500 and for Australian corporations at their national awards events and other gala occasions.

Simon Marnie is host of the popular *Weekends with Simon Marnie* on 702 ABC Sydney radio. Simon has been in radio for almost twenty years and started off life at Triple J. He has worked in community and commercial broadcasting, both behind the scenes and in front of a microphone. Simon has also conceived and produced SBS TV's *nomad*, as well as reporting for ABC Television's *TVTV*.

Lyndey Milan is the food director for *The Australian Women's Weekly* and co-host of Nine Network's *Fresh – Cooking with The Australian Women's Weekly*. Lyndey is the immediate past president of the Food Media Club of Australia. She is also Chair of the Fine Foods Committee and a councillor of the Royal Agricultural Society of New South Wales. In addition to being a fine speaker, Lyndey is well known and well loved for her passionate debating skills.

Tania Nash is an educator with over a decade of experience in speaking and presenting workshops. After completing a Bachelor of Applied Science degree majoring in Parks and Recreation, she opted for a complete change of pace and has worked predominantly in the food world, where she has spent the last fifteen years educating and entertaining people.

Ian Ross, Channel Seven's nightly news presenter in New South Wales, has had over thirty-seven years in television. He started work in radio at 2GB, before heading for the surf and 2MW Murwillumbah, and then back to 2SM in Sydney, before joining Channel Nine as a reporter and newsreader. Before his recent move to Channel Seven, Ian was news anchor with the *Today Show* on Channel Nine for eleven years.

Adam Spencer is the co-host of Triple J's *Breakfast Show*. He is also the author of *Adam Spencer's Book of Numbers*. With an almost-completed PhD in Pure Mathematics, Adam has been a popular fixture on the ABC TV science scene for quite a few years, hosting *Quantum* and the summertime science panel discussion show *FAQ*.

Marlene Vaughan is a speaker and singer. She is past president of the Savoy Arts Company and regularly appears in that company's productions of Gilbert and Sullivan operas. She is also a teacher of presentation skills and drama. She holds a Bachelor of Arts in Drama and English Literature.

PART 1

TEN STEPS
to Successful
PUBLIC
SPEAKING

STEP 1

PRELIMINARY PLANNING

We think in generalities, we live in detail.

ALFRED NORTH WHITEHEAD, *British mathematician, logician and philosopher, 1861–1947*

Learn how to create a mind map, identify the style of your speech, research your audience, and determine the essence of what you want to say, that is, the central theme of your speech.

As the son of a drama teacher, John Travolta, star of the cult movie *Pulp Fiction* and many other movies, does not subscribe to the 'off-the-cuff' inarticulateness that is frequently seen at Hollywood award ceremonies. He never stands before an audience to speak without preparing thoroughly beforehand. On *The Oprah Winfrey Show*, he admitted that it took him several weeks to plan, write and rehearse his acceptance speech to an invitation to pilot a Boeing 727 jet around the world as a Qantas ambassador.

While I was training in home economics, I was lucky enough to watch a leading Australian chef giving a lecture and demonstration on the art of making a good veal stock. Most of us students were slightly amazed that a three-hour lecture could be taken up by a simple stock-making demonstration.

The chef explained that producing quality stock was pivotal in creating sauces par excellence and impressed on us that, while it was not difficult to make, it required due diligence in following the necessary steps needed to achieve it. He started the demonstration by putting a rack into the base of a very large pan to keep the bones of veal knuckle, beef shin, chicken necks and wings from sticking to the bottom of the pan. Then he covered the bones with water and put the pan on a low heat. As it slowly heated a grey scummy mixture bubbled menacingly to the top and with a shallow spoon the chef skimmed the scum from the surface. As he skimmed, he kept on repeating that a good stock was the starting point of many dishes and 'that while the preparation may seem time-consuming and tedious the end result is well worth the effort'.

When eventually no more scum appeared, he added to the stock an onion studded with a few cloves, a clove of peeled garlic, chunks of carrot, celery and a string-bound bouquet garni. He brought all this to the boil and then reduced it to a simmer. By then the stock was starting to give off delicious aromatic smells. It was to be left to cook for five hours before being ready to be strained twice through a fine sieve.

Like all good demonstrators, our chef had a stock prepared beforehand so that we could appreciate the process of the final sieving. The final stock was a glossy, viscous elixir. To really make the lesson sink in he made us taste a stock from a packet and compare it with a taste of the real stock. The proof of the stock was in the sipping and he converted us all that day.

The moral of the story is that there are no shortcuts to making anything worthwhile. If you want to deliver a quality speech, you have to do the preliminary preparation. Before you can enjoy the thunderous ovation you will receive when you deliver your gems of wisdom from the lectern, there is always the necessary work that you have to do beforehand to achieve it. It does not matter whether you need to make a substantial presentation for your work, are invited to speak at a major conference, or have been asked to make a short speech at a friend's wedding, you will need to put aside the time to prepare your message.

If you have something important to say and put value on your thoughts and words, then you must give yourself every chance of succeeding. Preparation and more preparation is the primary key to success in any speaking situation. It is very difficult to speak off the cuff unless you have chalked up quite a lot of public speaking mileage and have regular opportunities to speak out.

Writing and presenting a speech is very much like making a great meal, 90 per cent of endeavours are in the preparation and 10 per cent in presenting the final dish to guests. The pay-off is the 10 per cent of effort when guests clean their plates and show their appreciation and approval.

All preparation is for a very worthy cause – so that you can bask in that magic 10 per cent peak when your approval rating goes off the scale. The trick is to enjoy the preparation just as much as the presentation.

CELEBRITY TIP

First and foremost – be prepared. It is impossible to be 'over-prepared' for any speech or public oration. It is a live performance. You can't go back and do a re-take. It has to be right the first time. So please treat it with care and respect.

IAN ROSS

The preliminary steps that will give you the strong foundation for your speech are planning or mapping your speech, defining the 'style' of speech you want to give, understanding the importance of identifying your audience and identifying the central theme of your talk.

Plan or map your speech

Plan your work, work your plan.

ANONYMOUS

If you are looking for a technique to make planning your speech easy and effective, try a technique called 'Mind Mapping'. I find mind mapping the best method for bringing my creative and logistical thoughts together. Mind mapping originated in the 1960s with Tony Buzan and allows you to generate a dynamic explosion of ideas. This mapping gives you an overview of your topic, enables you to plan routes and make choices, encourages problem-solving and helps you to work efficiently.

To create your mind map you will need a large sheet of blank paper, A4 size, used landscape fashion.

- Write the topic of your speech in the upper middle of the sheet. Don't put a frame around this title; instead use coloured pencils or pens to write over this until the topic leaps out at you.
- Then draw three thick, short, wavy branches emanating from the top of the title. The subtitles to be clearly written on these three branches are Style, Audience and Central Theme. Then draw four more thick branches to the side and bottom of the title. These can be subtitled Resources, Body, Introduction and Conclusion.

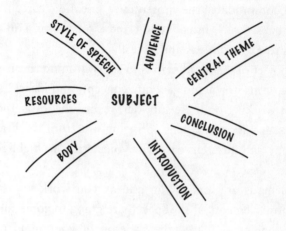

FIGURE 1: A BASIC TEMPLATE FOR YOUR MIND MAP

FIGURE 2: AN EXAMPLE OF A MIND MAP IN ACTION

- Normally in mind mapping the subject is central on the paper but the configuration described here should allow you to accommodate the potentially meatier categories of Resources, Body, Introduction and Conclusion, and allows room to expand ideas and notes.

The object of the mind map is to set your mind free to word-associate, brainstorm and generate concepts and ideas. Later, as you start working on these subtitles, record the ideas, thoughts and facts as subsidiary lines springing out from the branches. Use colour and different cases for your letters to highlight and punctuate ideas.

Mind maps are lots of fun and as you work you can see clearly how elements of the speech are going to come together.

Now, having prepared the skeleton of your mind map or planning, put that aside until you have identified the style or purpose of the speech you are going to make.

Decide on the style of your speech

I use the term 'style' generically – it means the overall purpose of the speech as received by your audience. While this step may seem obvious, don't undervalue it. The style clearly flags the direction for your speech.

Identifying the appropriate style is a simple exercise that will take you a minimum amount of time but should not be overlooked, as it is important in the overall planning of the speech. The style provides the focal point around which you organise your thoughts and planning, and helps you to focus on the manner of delivery and content.

There are six styles of speeches: to influence, to convince or lobby, to inform, to entertain, to inspire or motivate, and to sell an idea. The choice of styles is fairly clear-cut, making your selection easy. However, 'to influence' and 'to convince or lobby' are styles with close similarities, so you will need to understand the subtle differences between them to do justice to either style.

To influence

'To influence' is a style of speech used for situations when you need to persuade the audience that your ideas or opinions are the way forward. Your speech should explain the benefits and features of your idea. This is not a time to hard sell, but rather to provide the audience with anecdotal, soft facts and positive, epiphany moments. This style would be best suited to the front-runner in an ongoing campaign or a desire to promote a cause, project or person.

By articulating your understandings or your opinion of the issue or topic, you want to open up the audience's minds to the possibility of a different and valid viewpoint.

To convince or lobby

'Convincing or lobbying' is a more serious style of speech used to lobby for political or social changes. Although similar to the 'influence' style, delivery and content need to be stronger and punchier. Political 'great' Winston Churchill once said: 'If you have an important point to make, don't try to be subtle or clever. Use a pile-driver. Hit the point once. Then come back and hit it again. Then hit it a third time – a tremendous whack!'

With this style of speech, the audience will be confident that you have given them a positive statement of opinion. Your speech should be well informed about the case for and against the debate and conclude with a call to action.

To inform

Informative speeches set out to educate or provide credible and accessible data to your audience. You need to know your facts and present them in a logical and accessible manner. Summarise the important points in your concluding remarks.

Your audience should feel that they have been well informed and have gained new knowledge from listening to you.

To entertain

While all speeches should have an element of lightness to add dimension, an entertaining speech is normally an after-dinner speech, a celebration-event speech or a 'roast'. This style encompasses rib tickling – 'let me come up for air' – humour through to a lighter character of speech that invokes pleasurable smiles and the odd random chuckle. While only professional comedians can successfully present full-on humour, many of us can deliver a pleasing and entertaining speech that leaves the audience pleasantly surprised. Humorous anecdotal material and clever one-liners work well in this style of speech.

An entertaining speech will be appropriate, pleasing and humorous to the target audience.

To inspire or motivate

Inspirational or motivational speeches can include workshops, extended conference presentations or testimonial speeches.

Workshop and conference presentations are often given by professional speakers and trainers who specialise in this style of presentation and have honed their expertise over and over again until they perfect their performance. These types of presentations demand high energy and an ultra-confident presentation. Presenters use audience interaction and consequently need to be experienced and flexible to manage this effectively. It also requires the presenter to have a broad and sensitive understanding of their audience.

The desired outcome of workshop or conference presentations is that the audience will have confidence and belief in the presenter and therefore will be able to learn effectively under their tutorage. The audience should be left with the feeling that they have the tools and techniques that will enable them to make a positive change, as well as being left with sufficient adrenalin buzz to make it all happen – 'If he/she can do it, so can I'.

A note of caution for the new presenter: I recommend avoiding the workshop presentation as this would be too much of a challenge at this early stage of your speaking career. You will need some good quality experience or training before considering this level of presentation.

A testimonial speech might include telling your personal story of achievement or it can be a tribute to another person. It will need to be told emotively, 'straight from the heart'. It should be accurate, honest and sincere to effectively capture the audience's compassion and understanding. It should leave the audience wanting to go out and change the world, or even better, themselves.

To sell an idea

Presentations where you need to persuade the audience that your idea is the one to buy need to be slick, dynamic, to the point, influential and convincing, as well as tailored to meet the client's needs. Visual aids such as graphics, video, PowerPoint or other illustrative equipment can help convey the message. Conclude your speech by summarising the features and benefits of your presentation. Then remain quiet and wait for the audience to speak. Remember the old selling adage: 'He who speaks first has lost the sale'.

The desired outcome is an audience 'sold' on your idea.

On your mind map you can now fill in the style of speech you are going to make. Things are looking good. You have established the purpose of your speech and now it is vital to know whom you are going to be addressing.

Know your audience

Those in the cheaper seats, clap; the rest of you rattle your jewellery.

JOHN LENNON, *Royal Command Performance, 1963*

The advertising, marketing and commercial industries spend several billions of dollars each year in market research. Market research is vital to the success of any enterprise and most companies will not make any decisions until they have substantial data from telemarketing or specific focus groups. Research has become such an integral part of marketing and branding that companies go to considerable lengths to secure the right data. For example, the New York-based office of one famous Japanese car maker reportedly has 650–800 employees who spend their days researching the marketplace. This vital work of sifting and analysing information gives the company clear directions of what consumers want or need from a car. This research then enables the car designers and engineers to produce the ultimate driving experience for their target markets and hence increase their market share.

The world is constantly changing. What was socially acceptable a decade ago is different today and will be different again tomorrow. Businesses need to understand their market's expectations, how consumers live, how they think, what appeals to them and what doesn't. Armed with this information the company can then target campaigns or products to specifically meet these needs.

Your market is your audience, so it is just as necessary to do your own research to find out the dynamics of this group of people and what their expectations are. If you do not have a broad understanding of who makes up your audience, how do you know how to pitch your speech? It is common sense to investigate the profile of your audience. How do you begin to find out about the background of the people with whom you are going to communicate?

Start your investigations by talking to the organiser of the event or the person who wrote the invitation, as well as any other people you know are associated with the event. Most organisers will welcome you asking about the audience. It shows them that you are taking control of your session. They may not have a complete breakdown of the audience until close to the closing date for a conference or event but they will certainly be able to tell you the target market when the invitation is extended to you. This gives you the broad picture, which you will be able to tighten when you have the closing profile of the audience make-up.

You need not stop your research here, you can do your own investigations. If possible talk to the people who will be attending the meeting and ask them what their expectations are of the event. If you are speaking to an organisation or company have a look at their corporate profile on the Internet or access it through their corporate communications department. If you are speaking at a conference, review the program and see how your presentation will be affected by time of day, previous speakers' subject matter and any other factors that are going to impact on the audience's ability to focus on your message.

CELEBRITY TIP

Preparation is all-important for any speech. First, know your audience, how large it will be, who they will be, what they will be expecting and how many there will be. Make your speech relevant. It is vital to connect with your audience as soon as possible. This can be done with humour early on in your speech – as long as what you say *is* funny, appropriate and not possibly offensive.

LYNDEY MILAN

As an organiser of conferences and seminars I am required to collate results of exit surveys. Conference delegates are always asked for their comments and they give them willingly, especially if a speaker has really communicated their message well. Their comments also speak volumes about speakers who have not. Regardless of the speaker's profile or how clever the speech, audiences do not tolerate speakers who are obviously out of tune with their audience and have not made the effort to understand their needs, have not prepared sufficiently, or go over time.

> *Audiences do not tolerate speakers who ... have not made the effort to understand their needs, have not prepared sufficiently, or go over time.*

Some pitfalls of failing to understand your audience

A speaker at a retail service conference was a well-known celebrity. He is a very good speaker with valuable information to share. His signature style is very direct and to the point. Most audiences tolerate this style as part of the character and authority of this particular person and, indeed, some people find it quite intoxicating. He was addressing an audience of consumer relations managers, people who spend their working days dealing with less than compliant people. In his session he did not temper his manner of delivery, but was just as forthright and bombastic as normal. The audience found his style inflexible and arrogant. A large majority of the audience hated his presentation and documented this freely in their comments afterwards. If the speaker had researched his audience he could easily have softened his hard-line style and won them over.

An eminent university professor presented a paper to an audience of industry managers in exactly the same manner that he would present to his students. The audience, professionals in their field, were looking for a different level of information and were distinctly uncomfortable with the speaker's patronising manner. Instead of the presentation being a rewarding experience for them it had the opposite effect. If the speaker had taken pains to understand his audience he certainly could have delivered the style of presentation required.

There is an arrogance about any speaker who does not take into consideration the needs of his or her audience. Even though you have an idea of the group that you are speaking to, it is always useful to dig a little deeper to find out how the group is made up.

For example, imagine you have been invited to speak to the local Rotary group. You take into account that the object of Rotarians is to give service to the community and their members are drawn from local businesses. The average age of these people will probably be in the forty to fifty-five age bracket and it can be safely said that they are community-minded and share a common vision. This type of information gives you an excellent start and often this will be sufficient for you.

But imagine if the dynamics of the meeting were changed by the fact that this meeting is a promotion for new membership, not only for Rotarians, but also for the much younger market members of Rotaract. Maybe the style of speech you have prepared would have done very well with the older, slightly more conservative group, but will it work with the younger, more free-thinking crowd? Researching thoroughly and gaining a good understanding of the make-up of the audience is essential homework.

It all comes back to the importance of preparation. The more conscientious you are at this stage, the less risk of failure.

Remember, everything you can prepare in advance is going to work in your favour, which takes us on to the next step in the preliminary planning stage of your speech.

CELEBRITY TIP

It's vital to find out all relevant background information to give you a clearer idea of *whom* you are talking to. For instance: How many people are there? What do they do? Do they know each other? If in a group, what have they done that day? What are the clear objectives of your client? Should it be a relaxed or formal presentation? What time is required? What is the size of the venue? What equipment is available (lectern, video screen)?

This information will help guide you with your approach to speaking to and addressing the audience.

DEBORAH HUTTON

Identify your central theme

Determine what specific goal you want to achieve. Then dedicate yourself to its attainment with unswerving singleness of purpose.

PAUL J. MEYER, *author and founder of the Success Motivation Institute*

Intrinsic to any speech is the heart of the speech. I call this the 'Central Theme'. It can also be called the premise, the core message, the key idea, the nub of the oratory, the core or the essence of the speech, or the mission statement. This key communication can be summed up in one sentence that expressly conveys to you the essence or spirit of the message you are trying to convey to your audience.

Identifying your central theme is pivotal to the effective planning of your speech, whether your speech is two minutes or twenty in duration.

The importance of identifying the central theme

- The central theme keeps all your planning on track and acts as a litmus paper for any support material. It is the frame or skeleton that dictates the other materials to be used in the speech.
- The central theme need not actually be stated in so many words within the speech but nevertheless its essence should run stridently throughout the speech and your audience should be able to recognise and appreciate this central idea.
- The central theme also assists in the editing of your speech. Often when you collect material for the speech you become enamoured with some elegant prose you have conceived or some 'must-have' information. To judge how relevant it is to the effectiveness of your speech consider if it resonates with your central theme summary.
- The central theme helps the audience receive your message and know instinctively where you are heading. It also means that your audience will be more comfortable with your speech because they know clearly where you are heading and what you are saying. Audiences draw comfort from knowing what the speaker is doing and if they are comfortable they are receptive.
- The central theme stops the speaker being vague, confusing or going off on a tangent. These are tendencies that distract an audience.

When you first define that central theme, the mapping of your speech becomes so much easier. For example, Martin Luther King delivered his epic address 'I have a dream' to the American nation on 28 August 1963. This moving oration has been recorded as a defining moment in history when the eloquence and emotion of one man's words initiated social changes beyond black Americans' wildest expectations.

The style of speech was 'to inspire and motivate'. The central theme can be clearly understood and interpreted as 'Freedom and civil liberty for all men, pursued with dignity and discipline'. This clear premise gave a powerful and logical beacon to the writer as he was crafting the speech using the materials of political points, factual information and emotive rhetoric.

Choosing a style: some examples

- Your position at work means you are the person who has to give the speech at a retirement party. Considering the occasion, the audience and the recipient, the style of speech would be 'to entertain', the central theme could well be 'a gracious review of the person's company service and a light-hearted look at their retirement potential'.

- As a mother, you have strong views about nutrition and the access your child has to quality food choices in your child's school canteen. The opportunity comes to voice your concerns at the P & C Association. This is something that you are passionate about and your speech is an opportunity to promote change in the school canteen's approach to healthy eating. The style of speech could be 'to influence' or 'to lobby' and the central theme might be 'to motivate the P & C Association to adopt a school nutritional policy that will give our children healthier food choices'.

- As president of your local service organisation you have to present a report at the club's annual general meeting. The mechanics of preparing this report are the same as for preparing any speech. The style will be 'to inform' and the central theme is 'to give members a strong understanding of all activities and their outcomes in the past year and what to anticipate in the coming year'.

- You have been invited to speak on nursing as a career choice to HSC students. As the target audience is students who will be considering their future career your style would be 'to inform' and the central theme 'to give a broad understanding of career nursing opportunities and what steps they need to do to achieve a nursing position'.

To stay on track and deliver a clear, well-crafted speech that your audience can relate to every step of the way, make sure you carry out all of the defining steps: create a plan, decide on the style of your speech, find out about your audience and identify your central theme. These preliminary steps will make the fleshing out of the speech so much easier. They are simple steps and will give you powerful results.

STEP 2

KNOW THE BASICS

In any enterprise, it is not the nature of the problem that's important but the goals we fix, and the method we use to achieve those goals, which determine our success or failure.

ANONYMOUS

Learn about the basic structure of a speech and how to use this framework to develop your speech. This chapter also gives you some pointers in identifying and locating the appropriate resource material to support your speech.

Create a structure for your speech

The structure or bare bones of a speech or presentation should comprise an introduction, a body and a conclusion. The introduction should contribute 10 per cent of the speech time, the body 85 per cent and the conclusion 5 per cent.

The order in which you put the speech together is up to you and will depend on the way you like to process information. Some speakers start with the body of the speech and find that the introduction and conclusion follow easily. Others may find that the introduction or conclusion leaps out at them and then work on the body of the work. No matter which way you work, your speech should have a powerful opening, an arresting body and a strong conclusion.

Introduction

If you think about the opening lines of a book, you know they have to catch your attention. For example, you cannot help but keep reading after opening lines like those below:

> *She heard a knocking, and then a dog barking. Her dream left her, skittering behind a closing door. It had been a good dream, warm and close and she minded. She fought the waking.*

ANITA SHREVE, *The Pilot's Wife*

> *Imagine a ruin so strange it must never have happened. First, picture the forest. I want you to be its conscience, the eyes in the trees.*

BARBARA KINGSOLVER, *The Poisonwood Bible*

The introduction to a presentation or speech, while not necessarily as literary as the written word, should be equally as captivating. The opening lines of your speech are crucial in setting the scene. They encourage the audience to relax and make themselves ready to be engrossed in your presentation. An introduction should always be strong, appropriate, and to the point.

There is a school of thinking that says the introduction should 'tell the audience what you are going to tell them', the body of the speech should 'tell them' and the concluding part of the speech should 'tell them what you have already told them'. This is not a bad formula in making sure that the message is communicated well, but use this advice subtly and creatively rather than blandly summarising the core message.

An introduction is what it says – an opening or overture to the main part of the speech that gives you the opportunity to set the scene for the rest of the speech. If it is done well you will receive a positive response from the audience, giving your confidence a boost as you cruise through the rest of the speech.

SOME USEFUL INTRODUCTIONS

- **Get straight to the point.** Begin with a strong, creative statement that defines or leads neatly into your central theme.
- **Qualify your experience.** Although you may have been introduced by the emcee, it may be appropriate to qualify your presence at the event. Expanding on your knowledge or experience enables you to neatly come to the central message (or tell them what you are going to tell them) of the speech in a relevant fashion.
- **Begin with an anecdote or story.** Everyone loves humour or a good story so if it is appropriate to the topic and to the audience use your anecdote in the introduction, as it will help the audience relax and get ready to enjoy your presentation. Depending on the time available, a humorous anecdote or story is an excellent icebreaker. An anecdote or story breaks down any barriers between you and your audience – they may sit en masse but you need to communicate with them individually.

- **Avoid hackneyed openings** such as 'On my way to the meeting tonight' or 'Unaccustomed as I am to public speaking', unless you are a natural comedian and can put a topical or contemporary spin on these punch drunk lines.
- **Quotations** are always useful, especially if they have strong relevance to the audience, the subject, or are topical and the scope of the quote allows you to move strongly or humorously into the central message. Quotes used in the introduction should be punchy, short, topical or classic. It is even better if these quotes have become household phrases and your audience is one step ahead of you.

Some examples might be:

There is no such thing as a free lunch.

MALCOLM FRASER, *Australian prime minister, 1975–83*

In the year 2000, no child will live in poverty.

BOB HAWKE, *Australian prime minister, 1983–91*

I did not have sexual relations with that woman.

BILL CLINTON, *United States president, 1993–2001*

Frankly my dear, I don't give a damn.

RHETT BUTLER, from *Gone with the Wind*

The world is divided into people who do things – and people who get the credit.

DWIGHT MORROW, *American Senator*

Too bad all the people who know how to run the country are busy driving taxi cabs and cutting hair.

GEORGE BURNS, *American comedian*

- Or you might **parody** a well-known quote to make it stronger, more humorous or relevant to the topic.

INTRODUCTIONS TO AVOID

- The **pedestrian**. Don't launch flatly or unimaginatively into your message without bothering to do some lateral thinking to find a fresher and more dynamic way to phrase the opening.
- The **pretentious**. Don't try to be something greater than you are. The audience can be disenchanted with a long list of your achievements. Keep your CV details to relevant detail.
- The **grovel opening**. Don't open your speech with an apology such as 'I'm sorry I am not used to speaking in public so I will ask you to bear with me …', 'I am really nervous tonight, so please be kind with me'. While voicing this fear may relieve you, the speaker, there is every chance the audience will be distracted from hearing the full impact of your message. They could possibly feel a little anxious about your performance or even worse experience a gut-level reaction of feeling slightly exploited. Anything that interferes with them experiencing the message means that the message loses its effectiveness. Most speakers are nervous, most audiences are supportive but they do not want to know, or need know, that you are anxious.
- The **indecisive opening**. This type of introduction goes everywhere but does not flag the central theme message clearly enough for the audience to understand where they are being taken. The audience will become very uncomfortable and you can safely say you will have lost their interest very quickly.

Body of the speech

While the introduction is the teaser to set your speech in flow, the body of the speech is the powerful engine of your speech and provides the main feed of resource material of information, ideas and concepts. The body should constitute about 85 per cent of the speech.

This resource material can be in the form of an explanation, illustration, statistical data, anecdote or story, a comparison or quotations.

EXPLANATION

An explanation could consist of a straightforward explanation of a concept, such as the one below:

Since the 1985 discovery of the final resting place of the Titanic, damage caused by the number of underwater visitors has caused the ship to deteriorate rapidly. The Titanic sank in 1912, 325 miles (60 kilometres) off the coast of Newfoundland taking 1500 lives. I want to speak to you today about a proposed treaty to protect this historic wreck.

An explanation could also provide a springboard for the structure of the entire speech by using the 'why, how and who' of a subject. Using an explanation in this manner would incorporate a range of different support material such as anecdotes, statistics, illustrations, comparisons and quotations. For instance, if you are presenting a case study about managing a bed-and-breakfast venture, the introduction might cover why you became a B & B operator. The body of the speech would explain the benefits and features of owning a B & B business. The 'how' would include an overview of the work involved to keep guests happy, the marketing and promotion of the business. The 'who' would include information on B & B associations, trade shows and how to use these to advantage.

ILLUSTRATION

An illustration is an example that helps clarify any point. For instance, imagine you are presenting a paper at a conference and want to make a very strong point on the necessity of upgrading WorkSafe regulations for the building industry. You could illustrate this by citing an actual occurrence where the current regulations had failed.

STATISTICS OR FACTS

Statistics or facts might be numerical data or credible facts. Take care when using hard data in a speech. The data *must* be reliable and appropriate. Also be conscious that an audience's attention span is limited, especially when it comes to soaking up facts and figures. For example, if you are addressing a parent/teacher meeting about the risks of childhood obesity and the need to encourage children to exercise, you will need to provide current figures and facts to support your premise.

ANECDOTE OR STORY

Anecdotes or stories can include personal or first-hand experiences or may be based upon other people's anecdotes or stories. The first example below uses an anecdote about somebody else; the second uses personal experience.

You are giving an after-dinner speech to an audience of dairy farmers. You start the speech with this anecdote:

> *Six-year-old Grace, the daughter of a dairy farmer, watched in awe as a young mother breastfed her baby. Seeing her fascination, her father explained that this was a natural process in the animal world and for human babies as well. Grace listened carefully but still appeared a little anxious. 'But Dad,' she cried, 'is it pasteurised?'*

You are presenting a workshop on personal development. As you present all the components of the learning experience, you tell the story of your own growth and how you have overcome obstacles that have challenged this path of self-discovery. This helps qualify your authority and allows the audience to relate to you.

COMPARISON OF FACTS OR INFORMATION

You are addressing a meeting of consumer-relations advocates. You are talking about trends in the marketplace and how retailing has changed over the past decade. You compare the past retailing profile with today's situation and then forecast future trends.

QUOTATION

When using a pertinent quotation, always quote the author and, if appropriate and possible, the source. For example, imagine you are the bride's best friend and have been asked to make a speech at the wedding. The majority of your speech is spent commending your friend's virtues to the guests. You want to weave in the odd quote to change the pace and add some humour. Maybe you would choose one of the quotes from the group below to add to the mix:

In Hollywood, brides keep the bouquets and throw away the groom.

GROUCHO MARX

Marrying a man is like buying something you've been admiring for a long time in a shop window. You may love it when you get home, but it doesn't always go with everything else in the house.

JEAN KERR

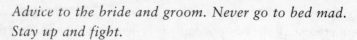

Advice to the bride and groom. Never go to bed mad.
Stay up and fight.

PHYLLIS DILLER

When you have amassed all the bits and pieces of appropriate resource material, you may find that you have more than you can effectively use. It is better to recognise this early rather than to craft your speech using all the material, only to find your speech goes way over time.

However tempting the material seems, try not to pack in too many concepts or real pieces of information – this is unquestionably a case of 'less is more'. A very rough rule of thumb is to use no more than four or five reasonably substantial different data or hard-core fact items in a ten-minute speech. If you are doing a longer presentation don't think you simply multiply the amounts of material items per ten-minute speech. You must review your timing carefully while you are developing the speech. Even in a thirty-minute presentation, too many hard facts, figures and information may leave your audience with glazed eyes. It is important that you leave time to lighten or strengthen the hard-core points you make with the use of anecdotes, stories or quotes.

Be objective as you read through what you have collected and then, using that 'red pen', edit ruthlessly. Disciplined editing makes for a much more potent speech. Question every piece: Does it pass the central theme litmus test? Is it key to the message? Does it provide contrast or texture? Is it relevant, powerful and/or does it fit in with the other material effectively? When you are ready to put it all together, choose material that will not only support your premise, but will allow each piece to organically flow from one concept to the next.

Conclusion of the speech

The conclusion is what it says – the finale of your work. This is the time when you weave the final words back into the essence of the central message. As you bring the speech to a close, it should leave your audience wanting more. The conclusion should be as strong as the introduction but shorter. The audience should be aware that you are preparing to close by a change of pace and texture in the concluding remarks. The conclusion should not take up more than 5 per cent of the speech.

SOME USEFUL CONCLUSIONS

- **A call to action**. Ask people to consider taking action in response to your presentation.

  For instance, if you are talking about your concerns about a proposed building development that will infringe on your golf club's car-parking facilities, your concluding remarks might call on all members to be united in their efforts to stop this: 'I urge you to sign this petition which will be sent to the local Council voicing our disapproval of these plans'.

- **A quotation** is always a good contender for a conclusion if you are at a loss for those final words. For example, you are speaking to a local community group about the lack of good city planning practice and how the city seems to be overgrown with ugly concrete box high-rise buildings. Once you have touched again on the message of your central theme, conclude with a good quotation: 'As American architect Frank Lloyd Wright once said: "The doctor can bury his mistakes but an architect can only advise his clients to plant vines"'.

- **Look to the future**. In this style of conclusion, you leave your audience with a hypothetical situation or question that will continue to spark their interest long after your speech is over.

   For example, you have been giving a presentation to clients hoping they will buy into the time-share apartments at a five-star resort. You want to leave these clients with a strong emotional appeal of why they should buy one of these apartments now. You have already vividly illustrated a picture of them playing golf on the immaculate eighteen-hole course, frolicking in the award-winning swimming pool with its water slides and body-surfing pool, working out in the fully equipped gym, leaving the children to have fun in the Kids Club and enjoying a candle-lit dinner for two in one of the fine restaurants. You conclude with these words: 'Put yourself in this picture – your family could be enjoying their next and best holiday ever – year after year after year'.

- A **rhetorical question** has a similar objective to the conclusion that 'looks to the future'. It is designed to make the audience think about the issues and topics you have raised in your speech.

   You are speaking to a group about environmental issues. You want to leave them thinking about the need for society to protect our fragile environment, so you conclude by asking the audience: 'Where do you sit on this issue – on the fence, or on the side of conservation?'

- **Summarise your central theme**. For example, if your central theme has been 'to raise awareness of the plight of orphan children in a third-world country with the objective of securing regular donations', your concluding remarks may be: 'As you have heard, these children have lost everything – their parents, their home and any comforts that this would have afforded them. They exist, they do not live a life filled with love and security like our children. If their story has touched you and you feel moved to make a difference in these children's lives, you can. Put your money where your heart is and make regular monthly donations to the – Fund.' (This example can also be seen as a call to action conclusion.)

CONCLUSIONS TO AVOID
- **Lengthy ones.** If members of the audience start putting on their running shoes, you have gone on far too long.
- **Endings that** give an expectation of conclusion but **don't finish.** They just keep on keeping on with phrases such as 'In conclusion', 'Finally', 'Let me say this before finishing' and 'Before I leave the stage I just want to finish on this note'.
- The **apologetic, overly grateful conclusion,** or what I call the 'Uriah Heep finish' – 'I just wish I could have said it better but I am grateful for your understanding and patience – thank you'. Do you really want the sympathy vote?

Identify and locate resource materials

The trouble with facts is that there are so many of them.

SAMUEL McCHORD CROTHERS, *The Gentle Reader*

In previous pages you have learned about the need to understand your audience, to define the style of speech, and to identify the central theme. You have seen how speeches need to be structured and you have started the mind mapping process. Now you need to seriously look at your resource material. Do you have sufficient material or will you need to do some research to strengthen existing components of your speech?

Invariably when you start putting pen to paper you realise that you need more detail, facts or data to support your case.

The object is to make yourself, as much as possible, an authority on your topic. You may not use all the information you gather but it will add to your understanding and knowledge of the subject and make the development of your speech easier.

As you have seen, this support material can be in the form of a definition, explanation, illustration, comparison, statistical data, published facts, testimony or quotes, comparison of data or anecdotal snippets.

So where do you start to find this right material for your speech? To narrow your search you need to identify the type of resource you want to make your speech convincing. The following information will give you some ideas on where to find this material.

Facts, figures and quotes

If you have an Internet connection this is the best place to start. You will find a vast range of information, facts, knowledge, theories and quotes by the bucketload. Whether you are computer literate and or not so computer literate this is the perfect vehicle for finding pertinent data.

If you would like to see a comprehensive list of search engines, look at the website <http://www.searchenginewatch.com>. They have lists of major search engines, directories, metasearch engines, paid listings, shopping searches, kids searches, specialty searches, country-specific searches and many more.

Each search engine has a help section to explain how to search with their particular search tool. Read it before you begin in order to maximise the effectiveness of your search.

AUSTRALIAN BUREAU OF STATISTICS

If you are looking for statistical information about Australia, the Australian Bureau of Statistics (ABS) is an absolute goldmine. It can provide information on demographics, the economy, health, the environment and social issues. ABS data is based on surveys and depending on what you are after, the information can be as recent as say within the past year or six months, or it may be up to four years old, if you are looking at the last Census survey. The surveys undertaken vary from monthly surveys through to annual and of course five years for the census material.

You can find information on their website at <http://www. abs.gov.au> , by phone, by visiting their offices or you can access this information from your State library. The ABS does provide free information services but there is a (small) cost involved if you wish to purchase specific reports.

STATE LIBRARIES

As well as providing ABS information, your State library can provide a wealth of information on a myriad of subjects.

Other resources

- Professional associations, chambers of commerce, state or federal government agencies as well as your local council are all sources of information. If you are looking for a specific agency, try the Internet first, then the telephone book.
- Major newspapers also have reference libraries for those wishing to find old newspaper editorials.
- Your local library is a perfect place to start your search. If you do not find what you need there, with the help of a friendly librarian you can work out where to look next.
- Look at reference books of all kinds. Take the time to fossick around in second-hand bookshops and at school and church fetes – you may find the odd gem of a book!

Anecdotes

Robert Menzies, while speaking at a political meeting, was interrupted by a woman who shouted: 'I wouldn't vote for you if you were the Archangel Gabriel!' 'If I were the Archangel Gabriel, madam,' replied Menzies, 'you would scarcely be in my constituency.'

The anecdote or story is simply the most efficient way to cement the point of your message. It allows you to reach the audience one on one. If necessary, take out some of your other material so that you can include an anecdote or story.

An anecdote or story is a very useful ingredient in speech-making as it can be a springboard to bring in key points. The right anecdote and story can also give that element of gentle humour that is so valuable in a speech. It humanises the presentation and softens the audience's response.

The length of your speech will determine the scope of any anecdotal material you use. Limited time means bite-size anecdotes, whereas the luxury of a longer presentation lends itself to a well-told story, especially if it relates to you and your experiences.

The beauty of an anecdote is that it does not have to strictly be your story and it does not have to be factual. Anecdotes are no one's exclusive property. Names, places, and subject matter can be changed to suit your needs. Some anecdotal stories lend themselves more effectively to provide the perfect introductory foil or line for your speech.

> *After a whirlwind courtship, the loving couple eloped and were married. After a few days the fact came out that the bride was a snake charmer. Slightly stunned by this revelation, the husband said reproachfully, 'How is it you never told me you were a snake charmer?' Said his bride, 'You never asked me.'*
>
> 2500 ANECDOTES FOR ALL OCCASIONS

The line 'You never asked me' gives endless opportunities for a smooth entry into your subject. For example, you might say: 'He may never have asked her but you'll be pleased to know I won't be so backward in giving you the facts ...', or 'I'm no snake charmer but I promise I will tell you everything you need to know ...'.

When using anecdotes, make sure that the anecdote is relevant to the flow of the speech. It should not be exploitative, that is, if it is grossly unfair or demeaning to someone, then do not use it. Don't use it if it makes you cringe, as it will surely make your audience cringe as well. Although an anecdote does not have to be based upon your own experience, it should be reasonably contemporary for the audience and within their lifetime frame of reference.

Where do you find these snippets that are going to give your speech that magic lift? You will find them in newspapers, magazines, books, on television and radio, and in everyday observations and conversation. Keep a file and notebook to record the items that capture your attention or are associated with your interests. Second-hand bookstores are also valuable sources of 'wit and wisdom'-style journals that often have the genesis of great anecdotes.

Language resources

CLICHÉS, PLATITUDES, IDIOMS AND METAPHORS

A word is not a crystal, transparent and unchanging, it is the skin of a living thought and may vary in colour and content according to the circumstances and time in which it is used.

OLIVER WENDELL HOLMES, JR

Language constantly evolves; phrases and words go in and out of vogue as new ones arrive on the scene. We probably flirt most constantly with the 'trendiest' and most prosaic words, until through constant usage they start to grate with our listeners. Once smart, these words and phrases then become predictable and banal.

According to the *Macquarie Dictionary* (third edition), a cliché is a 'trite, stereotype expression, idea or practice'. When I talk about clichés in this chapter I am not referring to a clichéd idea or observation on a topical issue. Such stereotypes are often cribbed from a media source. Often it is easier to keep in the swing of conversation by reiterating something that has been heard on a favourite talkback radio station. This mainly happens, I believe, because people do not have the time or interest to investigate the issue themselves. I am sure if you are presenting a speech on an issue or topic, you will have thought long and hard about how to represent your opinion. So let's discount clichéd ideas and observations.

However, most of us use familiar phrases or clichés in our normal communication. The trap with clichés is that they are comfortable and so they creep easily like 'old friends' into our everyday language until we become unaware that we are using a tired expression or idea. The cliché loses its effectiveness because its meanings can be ignored, overlooked or discounted. A speaker or writer who uses clichés is often viewed as lazy or slapdash.

The risk with clichés is that the integrity of message can be tarnished as the listener has heard the well-worn concept, phrase or expression to the point of deafness and the risk is that they may think your views are shallow and show no original thinking.

For example, how do you react to the following clichés?

I give my family quality time.

As the supermarket operator takes your money he says 'Have a nice day'.

A workshop leader promoting the importance of team-building says 'A chain is only as strong as its weakest link'.

'It was a defining moment,' said the staff member when she received a glowing review from her boss.

Recently I listened to a television football commentator who unwittingly and delightfully kicked from one cliché to the next in a short interview. If the team was not 'champing at the bit', they were 'second to none' and 'talking the talk and walking the walk'. There was a 'bit of a hiccup' but they 'managed to snatch victory from the jaws of defeat' and 'at the end of the day' 'were none the worse for wear'. Perhaps we worry too much about whether a cliché or phrase is acceptable when often a well-placed, succinct, but well-worn phrase perfectly rounds off what you are trying to say. No matter whether we are chatting to a friend or presenting in public we use clichés more than we imagine. For example: 'One thing for certain' in this 'day and age' is that many of us 'burn the candle at both ends' (or 'burn the midnight oil'), so that the 'bottom line' is a 'recipe for disaster' for our 'health and wellbeing'.

Other tricky phrases that pop into our everyday conversation are platitudes, idioms and metaphors. While the platitude is equally as dammed as the cliché, the idiom and metaphor are relatively acceptable to English-language purists.

The *Macquarie Dictionary* defines a platitude as a 'flat, dull, or trite remark, especially one uttered as if it were fresh and profound'. Examples might be 'As one door closes, another opens' or 'Better to have loved and lost than not to have loved at all'. Again according to the *Macquarie Dictionary*, an idiom is a 'form of expression peculiar to a language especially one having a significance other than its literal one'. Examples are 'at the drop of a hat' or 'to turn over a new leaf'. The *Macquarie Dictionary* describes a metaphor as 'a figure of speech in which a term or phrase is applied to something to which it is not literally applicable, in order to suggest a resemblance'. Examples are 'an open and shut case' or 'a sparkling personality'.

To the average person the difference between a cliché, platitude, metaphor and idiom is probably academic. If I say idiomatically that 'old chestnut' (meaning a tired old joke or overfamiliar subject) is not metaphorically 'my cup of tea' and if I platitudinise 'everything will be right on the night', I am conversing in well-worn phrases which would not be identified by the average listener as clichés, idioms or metaphors, but purely as phrases they have heard before. Very few people will stop to analyse the differences or care, but be cautious in your choice of expressions as opting to use a phrase that is overused and overworked will be recognised by your audience and may irritate the listener.

Personally I am tired of language police who very often want to 'throw out the baby with the bath water'. There is a richness in prose that incorporates a well-travelled or illuminative phrase that gives comfortable magic to any communication. So don't be afraid to use clichés, platitudes, idioms or metaphors if they give your speech more impact. For example, phrases such as 'suffocating crowds', 'the grace of a dancer', 'footloose and fancy free', 'paint the town red', 'human dynamo', 'over the moon' and 'long hot summer' offer word picture opportunities that can enhance a speech. A strategically placed and carefully selected cliché, idiom or metaphor can be used very effectively if it is delivered in a confident manner.

CLICHÉS AND PLATITUDES TO THINK TWICE ABOUT USING

Think twice about using clichés that are pretentious and might be seen as insincere by your listeners. A good rule of thumb is if it irritates you, it will more than likely irritate your audience.

Here are some current clichés and some that have stood the test of time. Check whether they may grate with your audience before using them.

> *cash cow, brain drain, time is money, you scratch my back and I'll scratch yours, survival of the fittest, the ball is in your court, at the present juncture, in my humble opinion, a clean bill of health, at this moment in time, not to worry, dog eat dog, the name of the game, benchmark, by the same token, I'll take that on board, do your own thing, firing on all cylinders, pull out all stops, coming on stream, the object of the exercise, take it or leave it, I kid you not, in the pipeline, to keep a low profile, a proven track record, to spell it out loud and clear, on the table, to lay it on the line, a whole new ballgame, Am I right or am I right?, a political minefield*

Vogue words

According to the authors of *The Right Word at the Right Time – A Guide to the English Language and How to Use It*, vogue words are 'words and phrases that suddenly come into vogue, to be heard in so many fashionable conversations and read in so many pretentious pieces of journalism. Vogue words are adapted either consciously as impressive sounding and "trendy" or unconsciously as a lazy and often imprecise way of conveying an idea.'

Vogue words are viewed just as disparagingly as clichés by the 'word police'. These are not newly coined phrases or words; they are words that suddenly and mysteriously come into fashion and become instant clichés. One that springs to my lips fairly readily (and I admit frequently) is 'absolutely'. I'm aware it is laziness to keep using 'absolutely' but it is so easy to answer with a positive and enthusiastic 'ab-sol-lutely'.

As with clichés, avoid vogue words when you can, especially if they sound pretentious to you or overworked. But if they fit the bill, use them. One totally undesirable expression that has 'stood the distance of time' is 'okay'. Many speakers and demonstrators use this as a transition word to move from one idea or activity to another. This is one word that should be cast aside, as 'okay' it certainly isn't!

Below you will find some vogue victims that you may wish to use or shun according to your needs.

24/7 (twenty-four seven), acid-test, blueprint, catalyst, chain reaction, charisma, clone, cutting edge, dichotomy, differential, double blind, end product, extrapolate, feedback, fellow traveller, flashpoint, geometrical progression, interface, leading question, logistics, overkill, parameter, psychological moment, quantum leap, rat-race, state-of-the-art, syndrome, task force, track record, winds of change, zero in on

---

Having established the style and central theme of your speech, in this step you have learned how to identify and locate information that will support your case. This collection of materials may include facts, figures, illustrations, anecdotes or stories and quotes which will add texture and depth to your communication. The body of your speech should use about

85 per cent of the time available to speak. You have grasped the need for a powerful introduction which should take up no more than 10 per cent of the speech and distinguished what makes a good, strong conclusion – no more than 5 per cent of the speech. Now you are ready to move onto the next step – 'The Construction' of your speech.

STEP 3

THE
CONSTRUCTION

By the work one knows the workman.

JEAN DE LA FONTAINE, *French poet and writer of fables, 1555–1628*

You have the plans; you have the materials. Find out how to put them all together.

I was watching a TV lifestyle program recently. It was a makeover of a garden that desperately needed it. The owner of the garden had been spirited away for a couple of days while the makeover team went to work. Having spent some time in central Italy, the owner had always wished to create a little piece of typical Firenze countryside in his backyard wilderness. So the theme was set and it was interesting to see how the plants and props were chosen.

The team had thoroughly researched the style of garden to discover the type of plants typical to that region that would grow in Australia. While pavers and the expected clay pots filled with geraniums were included in the garden, the authenticity of the selection of flora with its mixture of shrubs, bushes and flowering plants gave the garden real dimension. When they finished you could almost feel that over the back fence lay the rolling hills and plains of Tuscany.

It was obvious that the makeover of the garden was a carefully planned and researched project. During the course of the planning no doubt many plants, props and footage were discarded as not contributing to the end result.

The same guiding principle of stringent editing applies whether it is achieving a great lifestyle program, an epic film or writing a speech. You will collect a great deal of material, and much of that material will end up on the cutting room floor. As you saw in the previous chapter, less is definitely more when selecting support materials for the body of a speech.

You have to look at the balance and flow and use only the pivotal material that really supports the premise of your speech. It is a great temptation to cram every conceivable fact, figure and scrap of information into your speech because you have put in considerable work to reach this stage. But you need to recognise that any research you have done, whether used or discarded, is never wasted. Research gives you that edge of knowledge that is going to increase your confidence and understanding about the topic so it does not matter that you do not use all of it.

By now your mind map or planning will allow you to see easily the patterns and key issues that are emerging. As your message takes shape, you will be able to identify the best materials for your needs to make it into a homogenous whole and reserve the remaining detail for future reference.

The style of your speech (see pp. 8–11) will influence how you decide on material, so keep this in mind when making the final selection of resource material. Below are some guidelines about the sorts of material you should include in a particular style of speech. But, remember, this is a guide only; if you can see a more appropriate source, go for that.

To influence

For the 'influence' style, use positive illustrations, explanations, anecdotal or personal story lines and quality information material that highlights the benefits of your concept. Research sources from the Internet, newspapers, magazines or other publications. This is a softer sell than the 'convince or lobby' style of speech and you need to make the information as palatable and as broad as you can. Avoid intricate statistics and blood-pressure-raising data comparisons in this style of speech. You are wooing the audience rather than confronting them.

To convince or lobby

This is where you need to drive the message home in a convincing way, so use hard data, statistics, testimony or quotes, and comparisons of conflicting data. Remember, credible reference material is vital. You need to research thoroughly and double-check the sources. You need to consider carefully how you are going to present these facts in a logical but interesting order. Avoid disseminating these facts in a 'list'-style approach as this can be perceived by the listener as predictable. It indicates to the listener a lack of creativity in weaving facts and information into the narrative of the speech. There is still room for an anecdote or story to soften the approach.

To inform

You need to know your subject inside out and make sure you have all the facts you need, to present this style of speech well. Use any support material but remember – you want your audience to retain the information. The average adult has an attention span of ten minutes so information should be presented in a textured way to take this into account. This means not all hard facts – sandwich hard facts with lighter prose such as anecdotal material to illustrate the point.

To entertain

You don't need to rush for the joke book or whoopee cushion to give an entertaining speech (see After-Dinner or Humorous Speeches, pp. 231–243). Draw on your own or other people's experiences for humorous moments, allow your creativity and own humour to flow. Inadvertent humour can be found everywhere: on radio, television, in publications, in everyday life, as well in quotations. Quotes are a rich and valuable source of materials for the lighter speech. For example, if the speech is based on 'the so-called joys of exercise', consider how either of these two one-liner quotes could work effectively for you:

I like long walks – especially when they are taken by people who annoy me.

FRED ALLEN

The only reason I took up jogging is so that I could hear heavy breathing again.

ERMA BOMBECK

To inspire or motivate

If you are making a speech that aims to inspire or motivate (see Testimony, or 'tell your story' speech, pp. 226–228), you have to draw on personal experience, whether it is yours or that of someone close to you. This personal experience has to come from the heart; you need to focus on your story and how you are going to tell it. You are painting a picture in this style of speech, so choose your words carefully to allow your audience to see what you have experienced. Be honest: an audience will know if you fudge it. If you use any additional research material it must be absolutely pertinent and credible.

Workshop presentations (see pp. 194–205) need to be very carefully researched and need to provide high-quality information. To present a workshop also involves the need for interaction with your audience. The purpose of this interaction is to help them relax. That makes it easier for them to embrace the ideas and information that you are providing. Therefore the research you need for this type of speech will be multi-layered – not only will you have to consider how to make the information accessible and tangible to your audience, but any group activities you include should be chosen to maximise the impact of your message. Definitely use anecdotal and personal stories to anchor a point. Your presentation will need to pass stringent examination by an often sceptical audience. Not all successful speakers can present a workshop well, even those with extensive experience in speaking. Presenters who have a training or education background will probably find this style of presenting very rewarding.

To sell an idea

As there is always an emotive element in selling anything, target any motivational sentiments you can identify to make your speech relevant to your audience. This calls for you to thoroughly research the background of your audience. No matter how slick your presentation, it is no use trying to sell a campaign or idea or product if you don't know how to 'press their buttons'. Once you have established exactly who is your target audience, the support material will be easy to identify. Any use of facts and figures in this type of presentation needs to be immaculate.

How to begin, how to finish and how to fill in the middle

I would love to be able to give you a perfect formula for this step in creating your speech, but having spoken to many speakers, I have found that this step is a personal journey and each speech may throw up a different route to achieve this. There is no right or wrong way to do this, whether you start with that defining opening introduction, or focus on the body of the speech where the introduction and conclusion will leap out at you as you progress. A few bold and different speakers like to identify their concluding remarks first and work backwards. You need to experiment to find the best method for you.

Personally, I do not have a set format. Occasionally I have that 'light-bulb' moment that gives me the audience-grabbing introductory paragraph, but generally I find that by the time I have identified my style of speech, determined my central theme and collated all my material, a clear pattern emerges of how I will place this material in the speech. As I research my material I always keep an eye out for a strong introduction and conclusion. I find that I am so focused that I am practically halfway there as I start to write the outline of my speech, and it all seems to fall naturally into place.

I leave this all-important outline simmering in my mind for a day or so, then go back to it when I find it easy to edit. By reading it aloud I find I have a rough idea of timing. Reading aloud also makes editing much easier as you will find you often turn phrases into more comfortable prose. I leave it again for a period and then go back to it. I keep reading it aloud a few more times. This is where I start to see any further and final changes that I need to make. As the speech starts to really take shape in my mind I destroy the original outline, replacing it with key headings only. These key headings act as my memory prompts.

For me this is the most effective way of presenting a speech. I find by the time I have moved on to writing down those memory prompts I have thoroughly taken ownership of the speech. So much so that I can recall a speech from the memory prompts even if it is one that I made ten or fifteen years ago. Now this, coming from a person who cannot remember where she put her car keys, is testimony indeed!

The important thing is to experiment until you find the most comfortable and efficient way of metamorphosing all the planning, research and collating into your own personal style of speech. Be tolerant with yourself as you experiment. Believe in your capabilities to find the best method for your needs.

There are some key issues to remember when putting your speech together:

- Ensure that the elements of the speech – style, central theme, introduction, body and conclusion – are apparent.
- Edit your work by reading it aloud until you are absolutely comfortable with the flow and the language.
- Check that the speech fits within the required timeframe.

The benefits of reducing your speech to key headings means that you are not tempted to simply read the speech. This does not mean you have to learn the speech verbatim. By the time you summarise the speech into key headings it will have become a comfortable, flowing, second skin and these prompts will simply keep it running smoothly from one idea to the next.

Obviously there are times when speeches need to be read, but speakers who are chained to their written words are a distraction to their audience. Unless the speaker is very experienced and used to presenting straight from text or copy while maintaining good eye contact, it is a risky strategy for the novice speaker.

The inexperienced speaker is often fearful of losing their place and so their eye contact with the audience diminishes. Eye contact with your audience is vital in delivering a speech successfully (see Make eye contact, pp. 99–102).

If you feel that you need the security of the text of the whole speech, then a tip is to use coloured pens to highlight different chunks of prose/concepts/ideas so that you can easily see where you are. This reduces the chance of losing your place when you are making that valuable eye contact with the audience.

> *Eye contact with your audience is vital in delivering a speech successfully.*

How to weave in support material

Some traditional methods of incorporating resource material into a speech are to place it in chronological order, to use cause and effect, or to follow a journalistic approach with its who, when, where, how and why order. While this may have merit in certain speeches, for me, the all-important criterion about the placement of material is its ability to flow comfortably from one piece of data or anecdotal material onto the next. As you decide on the material, the priorities of key information will shape how you place it.

Do not restrict yourself by thinking you have to list information. If the placement of material is wrong and does not flow well, it will show up when you start rehearsing your speech. As you speak it aloud, you will soon see if you need to alter it.

Speaking the words out loud is much more beneficial than simply reading them. When you read you see no shade or depth. By vocalising your words, you shape the speech much more effectively. You can hear clearly when an idea doesn't work or a transition is not smooth. You become used to hearing your voice and connecting with your written ideas, your words, your voice. You can hear if there is a natural rhythm, a cadence that puts life into the collection of words you have so carefully put together.

When pulling your speech together, remember it is vital that each item of material links compatibly and plausibly with other material. Each supporting component should flow logically and intelligibly. When there is too much material there is a risk of it sounding like a list. Stringent editing will avoid this. Better to use fewer supporting elements and expand on these, than try to pack in too much information.

Bridges to the next concept

So how do you move from one idea to another, from one lot of data to statistics or from an anecdote to a quote? You need to use a linking phrase or sentence. Imagine you are speaking about healthy eating issues:

> *Nutrition messages today are confusing. We do not know whether we should predominantly be eating low-carb, moderate-fat or low-fat and moderate-carb diets. <u>To see if I could clarify this</u> I researched the latest findings from some of the world's leading university nutrition schools. Harvard's School of ____ ... <u>Interestingly</u>, at Sydney University ...*

As you can see in the above example, where the transition sentences and words are underlined, if there is compatibility in the material it is an easy task to flow from one concept to another. You will probably notice as you develop your speech that these transition words or phrases become second nature. At other times you may need to work at finding the suitable verbal bridge to take you smoothly into the next support statement.

I have provided the following link words and phrases, which are helpful as a starting point when trying to locate the right phrase. Some are a bit starchy but definitely useful!

> *After all ..., Alternatively ..., Another viewpoint is ..., As a result ..., As has been explained ..., But it's not*

all ..., But would you believe ..., Compare this with ..., Here is another way of looking at the issue ..., In any case ..., In light of what has been said ..., In view of this fact ..., Mind you ..., On the one hand ..., To balance the view ...,To support this ...

Preparing and managing speech notes

Signposts only show the road, they don't go along it.

SWISS-GERMAN PROVERB

I am always nervous whenever I see a speaker without notes. Often they are either completely unprepared and think they can wing it, or they have memorised their speech. Both ways are filled with hazards. The unprepared have no sense of where the speech is going to lead them and no sense of timing. Those who rely on their memories run the risk of forgetting what they are going to say, or are so wired they know the speech inside out and deliver it too dramatically. A balanced sense of theatre helps any presentation, but a full-blown, over-the-top presentation does not lend itself well to the public-speaking medium and will only make the audience squirm.

Audiences are most comfortable with a speaker who knows where they are taking the audience, who can deliver their speech in a confident and honest manner. If notes are used unobtrusively, the audience does not even notice.

Speaking to an audience is an intimate communication. You are seeking to reach them individually, as well as in their entirety. While there will always be an element of performing, including an awareness of stage presence and using your voice, face, and body language to convey a range of emotions, public speaking is all about connecting with your audience at a personal level rather than creating a theatrical flummery.

Speech notes are what you should have after hours of sifting, editing and rehearsing. They may be in the form of key headings that serve as memory prompters or they may be an entire scripted piece. As mentioned earlier, reading a speech challenges most speakers as they are tied to following it line by line, increasing the risk of losing their place when they look up for that vital audience eye contact. Only politicians, lecturers and very experienced speakers can do it reasonably effectively. It takes a great deal of practice to make it look seamless.

However, this is your performance and you must be comfortable and confident when you step up to speak, so use whatever form of notes will give you that inner security. If you can, use the memory prompters, because although they will probably push you outside your comfort zone, they will give your delivery that extra edge.

CELEBRITY TIP

Never read a speech. It's vitally important to know *what* you're going to say … highlighting key words and glancing down to keep on track is acceptable. Put the required hours in, go over and over it, remember what you're saying and deliver your speech as if it's just coming into your head for the first time.

If you're delivering a written speech, be sure to use a larger font and wide spacing between lines, highlighting important words or thoughts. I like to use a size 16 font in Arial with one and a half line spaces in between. It helps to keep your place when you quickly glance down.

DEBORAH HUTTON

Using memory prompters

- When the outline of your speech is complete and you are happy with it, as you start to rehearse you will find the key headings or words jump out at you as you move from one idea or snippet of material to another. Write down these headings separately.

- From now on as you practise your speech, use only these headings as a guide. As you rehearse you will see whether you need to use other subheadings or words to smooth out the memory process.
- Use either cards or standard DL-size envelopes to record your notes. Always use these horizontally and only write on the top half. Put a couple of headings on each card or envelope. This means it is easier for you to see when you are at a lectern or even if you are speaking without a lectern. Using the top half is important, as it will keep your eye level high, which means the notes are less obtrusive for the audience. Always number these notes so that if you drop them you can easily put them back in order.
- When you have rehearsed your speech and can move comfortably from each memory prompter to the next – destroy the outline. By doing this, you acknowledge your memory prompters provide all that you need to present. This act of taking ownership of the speech gives you confidence in your ability to deliver it well. Trust me – if you have done your work thoroughly, you will not need the security blanket of the outline.
- As you speak, move the notes to one side as you finish them or, if speaking without a lectern, move them to the back of the pack.

Using the full text

If you really feel insecure or there is just not enough lead time to achieve the level of comfort needed to use memory prompter headings, use a fully scripted speech. The following pointers should help to keep you on track:

- Print out the speech in the most effective font size. Big is beautiful.
- Print the text on the top half of the page only, so that your eye is not dragged downwards as you speak.
- Number the pages clearly.
- Use different coloured highlighters to identify different components of the speech. In this way you will be able to see clearly where you are at any stage. As you rehearse, practise lifting your eyes frequently to the imaginary audience.

You have learned in this chapter that there is no right or wrong order to assemble the speech. Some speakers find that the introduction or conclusion will leap out at them, while others will work through the processes until they find what suits their purpose. As you decide on the resources to use in the speech consider the different style of speeches as your chosen style will determine the most effective use of materials. As the speech, comes together and you write the outline, condense the chunks of prose or information down to simple memory prompters. If you do opt for the full text then make sure that you use all the simple techniques shown in this step to maintain your eye contact with the audience. You have produced the product; the next step is to make sure you 'Do It Your Way'.

STEP 4

'DO IT YOUR WAY'

*Do not be awestruck by other people and try to copy
them. Nobody can be you as efficiently as you can.*

NORMAN VINCENT PEALE, *The Power of Positive Thinking*

*Realise the benefits of being true to yourself in your language, gestures and
appearance. Read the audience's body language to help your performance.*

Finding *your* voice

What does it take to make a good speaker? Is it enough for you
to articulate well, present your facts well and perform capably?
Well, that certainly makes you a competent speaker but does
not necessarily make you a good speaker. The shift in the
audience's perception comes when you are able to communicate
your inner spirit or your genuine self. It is the ability to find
your own voice and be steadfastly true to yourself that will
make you a more dynamic speaker.

Having myself been through the dry mouth and sweaty palm stage, I appreciate that first-time speakers among you are wondering if you will even manage to get a word out, let alone be articulate, present facts and perform well. Be reassured that there have been many new speakers, who although lacking experience and the polished edge that comes with practice, still manage to completely capture their audience. When they speak from the heart and are true to themselves, the magic happens.

If you are reading this book you are obviously considering speaking at some stage. When that window of courage presents itself, go for it. Each speech you make after that becomes easier and easier.

Personality and charisma

Learn what you are, and be such.

PINDAR, *fifth-century Greek poet*

You don't need to be Einstein to know that there are different styles of presenters, from the showy through to the quietly confident, from the polished performer to the simple, straight-from-the-heart speaker, from the loud, ego-driven speaker to the humorous and self-deprecating. All have something to give and all have their charm. If there is any secret ingredient to speaking apart from preparation, more preparation and practice, it is to be true to yourself.

From the time we are young, we all get labels. We pick up and internalise the negative. From my childhood I remember family and neighbours saying what a shy, quiet child I was. I also had a draconian grandfather who thought I was a wimp of a child and told me so in many different ways. I tried on all these opinions for size, saw that they suited me, and so became that shy, quiet person for most of my young and adult life. Eleanor Roosevelt said 'No one can make you feel inferior without your consent'. Unfortunately, too often we consent. Having wasted so much time being something other than my authentic self, I am naturally against any outside influences that are going to define or confine an individual.

Rather than trying to analyse whether you are an introvert or extrovert, spend the time getting in touch with what you really want to say. Push aside the different forms of political correctness or insecurities which most of us suffer from – pinpoint your inner voice and have the courage to use it. This also means that the language you use must be yours, you must be comfortable with it. Forget the dictionary for prettying up that particular phrase or word. Don't try to be something other than what you are.

For me, charisma lies in the ability of a speaker to allow the audience into their emotional world – so that they can see them as they are, beauty spots, warts and all. Think of the success of a performer like the comedian Billy Connolly. Most of us would say that he is chock-full of charisma. Even though his language would normally offend many conservative people, that is totally overlooked as he invites us all to join him as he literally lays all things bare (including symbolically often being seen dancing naked like a child in some of his television epics). Billy Connolly is light years ahead of most of us in having the courage to be himself. What an example he is of the rewards of being truly in touch with his inner voice.

For many of us the difficulty lies in simply identifying what we think, let alone externalising it. We are so programmed to be polite, to keep our counsel, to avoid offending or contentious issues. Fear of failure and political correctness keep us bound – all those inner voices giving you sceptical messages: 'Who is going to listen to me?' 'What have I to offer?'

By being true to yourself and speaking out, I don't mean that you should be gratuitously contentious, unless of course it is an issue that is truly important to you and you accept the likelihood that other people's opinions may well differ from yours. But, for example, if you are presenting a lobby-style of speech you should realise that your passion will be pivotal in persuading your audience.

But is it worth taking the risk to be yourself, to be true to yourself? I guarantee that whatever style of speech you deliver, your authentic words will resonate with your audience much more than any fudged speech that is full of elegant prose and carefully crafted influences but delivered without soul. You cannot fool an audience; they will see through the counterfeit and view it as competent but lacking conviction.

Some of the great statesmen and personalities of the past century stand the test of time, remembered for their deeds and words. These people who changed the face of history understood the power and impact of an oratory spoken from their hearts. Think of how the following statements resonate:

Ask not what your country can do for you; ask what you can do for your country.

JOHN F. KENNEDY, *35th president of United States of America,*

in his Inaugural Address to Congress,1961

Never in the field of human conflict was so much owed to so few.

SIR WINSTON CHURCHILL'S *speech to the British parliament about the bravery of*

gallant airmen in the skies over England against the might of the German Luftwaffe, 1940

Well may they say 'God Save the Queen' as nothing will save the Governor-General.

GOUGH WHITLAM'S *statement after being*

dismissed as Australian prime minister,

11 November 1975

Push past all the negatives to get in touch with what you really think or feel, then be bold, have the courage to put these thoughts or ideas into your own words – throw away the dictionary and talk. Look at the style of language that these great statesmen used – no pretentious verbiage here; instead the prose is simple and direct.

How to get in touch with your inner voice

> *If man really knew himself he would utterly despise the ignorant notions others might form on a subject in which he had such matchless opportunities for observation.*
>
> GEORGE SANTAYANA, *philosopher and poet, 1863–1952*

For me the 'inner voice' is the essence of a person's values, principles, character and personality that allows them, without fear, to take ownership of their opinions. The inner voice is the authentic you.

A small number of lucky people are naturally in touch with this inner self, wearing their opinions and their social conscience on their sleeves, while the rest of us have buried it under layers of habit of social conditioning and not speaking our mind. How do we rid ourselves of these insecurities and find the courage to speak out?

Apart from considering years of therapy, are there viable alternatives to achieving this? Naturally it does depend on how fearful you are of having your opinions projected, nakedly and unashamedly. While acknowledging that there are no quick fixes to any change, I have found the following have helped me get in touch with my true persona. These solutions relate to general insecurities that many people experience; they are not intended as a panacea for any deep-seated problems.

- Mind mapping a specific problem is a terrific help in loosening ideas and thoughts.
- Passion or belief in a subject is always a sure-fire route to finding your 'inner voice'. Nothing is more motivating than a belief in a cause or a philosophical ideal. If that passion has dampened or you have lost the plot, you may have to do a bit a work on yourself.
- Focus is an important activity. When you focus your attention on something you make it happen. We are what we think. You need to allow the topic or fragments of an idea to consume you. Focus your attention on it whenever you can. This can be difficult when you have demands of work, family and social life but at every lull moment when you are exercising, sitting in traffic, going to sleep or waking up – focus your attention entirely on that inner voice. The solution will surface.
- Neuro-Linguistic Programming (NLP) has been described as a bit like an 'owner's manual' for the brain. For over twenty-five years, scientists, psychologists and other practitioners have studied successful people's behaviour and thinking. The results are a collection of information and techniques that enable individuals to access more of the true potential of their brains. I do recommend that you study books on the subject to learn more as NLP tools offer valuable insight and help to enable positive changes in behaviour and thinking. The book that helped me most was *The NLP Coach* by Ian McDermott and Wendy Jago.

NLP offers emotional and mind-changing strategies. It gives you some great tools like 'reframing' or 'anchoring' (see Anchoring, p. 94) to reach that happy inner core. I have found that 'anchoring' works really well for me.

'Framing' refers to how we classify experiences. 'Re-framing' is changing the frame (boundaries) or experience for the positive or different viewpoint. Or to put it into lay language, using a different perspective to look at things. A simple example is: 'The glass is half-empty'. Reframed, it becomes 'The glass is half-full'. Just switch that emotional frame to find the solution. If you are sitting there, staring into space, thinking that you are totally blocked and have absolutely no idea of what you want to say, reframe this by thinking 'If I did not have a block, what would I like to say?' This is an amazingly simple yet effective practice.

- A quick method that has worked well for me is my freewheeling version of Gestalt therapy technique. Gestalt therapy was originated by psychoanalyst Fritz (Frederick) Perls who wrote *In and Out the Garbage Pail*. His aim was to assist people in owning their experiences and developing a healthy 'gestalt' or wholeness. One of his techniques was to get his client to sit in a chair with a chair opposite, which represented the problem or blocked area. The client would then have to role-play both 'chairs' and talk out the problem. In my version I act out both roles and, even though I feel a little tentative and slightly absurd as I talk to an empty chair and then reply, the effort is well worthwhile as it crystallises my thoughts and ideas. So I recommend it to you. However, best to do it in the privacy of your own room!

- A daily meditation practice really helps release anxieties and if, while you are in the alpha state (brainwaves slow to what is identified as an 'alpha' state when you are in a reflective or relaxed state), you focus on self-belief affirmations and successful speaking, you will find solutions surface easily when you return to consciousness.

- If public speaking is to be part of your career journey and you are finding it hard to speak out, consider investing in life coaching sessions with an NLP-trained practitioner. A life coach is like having a super manager in your corner, who through planning, encouragement and review of your objectives, guides you to achieve personal success. An additional bonus if the life coach is an NLP practitioner is that coaching will no doubt make use of the NLP tools. These tools provide shortcuts for personal development which mean you will learn more quickly.

CELEBRITY TIP

Above all, *be yourself*. Please avoid taking on affectations or mannerisms you may have admired in other speakers. You will earn a lot more respect from any audience by doing it your way – warts and all!

IAN ROSS

Appearance

A tall drooping man who looked as though he had been stuffed in a hurry by an incompetent taxidermist.

P.G. WODEHOUSE, *The Mating Season*

I remember asking for a colleague's opinion of a speech I had presented and was amazed with the reply that she found my wearing jeans rather than a skirt distracting. This could, of course, be construed either that the speech was a complete non-starter and/or this person was rather conservative. However, it taught me a very good lesson in as much as I realised how much people do take account of the whole package. While I still wear jeans when speaking, I have certainly developed a more formal approach to my appearance when making a presentation.

Research has shown that appearance plays a vital role in others' acceptance of us. As a society we judge others by what they wear and how they take care of their appearance. We value people more when they have obviously taken care with their appearance and dress. We like clean hair, cared-for hands and fingernails, we love people to be clean and smell good and appreciate polished shoes. We admire others who have developed their own signature style. Our society pays obeisance to glamour – think of the megabucks that are paid to supermodels and how film stars reinvent their looks to recapture us. As Oscar Wilde said in *The Picture of Dorian Gray*: 'It is only the shallow people who do not judge by appearances'.

So if you want to be ahead of the game in our image-focused society, you need to consider how you look when you stand up to speak. There is no doubt that your audience will and they will start matching an emotional value to your appearance before you even open your mouth.

Key factors in dressing for accolades

- Appropriateness is the key, keeping the function or event or occasion very much in mind. Consider the type of occasion, its timing and, most importantly, consider the audience. For example, designer grunge may be perfect for the ad agency office, but when presenting to a new client you need to wear a 'meet-and-greet' style suit (unless of course the client is also into the grunge look). What you wear when making your point at the local P & C meeting will be very different from what you wear when giving an address at a school awards night. More casual clothes will be fine for the P & C Meeting but as an invited presenter at an awards night you will need to dress more formally. Both outfits should be given the same consideration – what suits you best, what makes you feel good and what gives you that important edge.

- Wear those outfits that other people compliment you on. Sometimes the outfit that you think makes you look good does not send out the same signal to the viewer. If in doubt, get a friend to guide you (not necessarily a partner, as they can tend to be biased or partner-blind).
- Clothing and shoes need to be comfortable. There is nothing worse than wearing something so tight you can hardly breathe. Your body needs to be comfortable so that you can breathe properly and move around freely.
- Dressing up for an occasion can give you an important psychological boost. It makes you feel good, gives a lift to your spirits and gives you more confidence. For example, once when I was feeling a little flat before a speaking engagement, I went out and bought myself some really flashy earrings. They were so outrageously big and bold that it made me smile just to think of them. Wearing them made me feel glamorous and that certainly gave my performance the up-beat boost that I needed. For men, how about a new tie or a flower in your buttonhole to achieve that euphoria?
- Always check your hair, teeth, face and clothing before speaking.
- If you wear glasses, and are not into contact lenses, make sure your glasses are anti-glare, contemporary in style and shape, that they suit you and are scrupulously clean. If you wear them, wear them; don't keep removing them to let them hang dangerously between your fingers, only to put them on again when you realise you cannot read your notes. It looks demented and if you drop the wretched things you, too, will feel demented.

Body language

> *Language emerged through bodily action before being*
> *codified into speech.*
>
> DAVID F. ARMSTRONG, WILLIAM C. STOKOE AND SHERMAN WILCOX,
>
> *Gesture and the Nature of Language*

The majority of us are sensitive to the subtle communications that body language gives us. We might not be able to read them correctly all the time but we do have an understanding at an instinctive level. A dismissive shrug, folded arms, nervous fingers pulling earlobes or touching the face, a welcome smile and open arms all pierce the comprehension of the recipient. When listening to others, we take in the whole person; we hear the communication not just with our ears but with our eyes and gut instinct.

Research has shown that the verbal part of communication constitutes only a minute 7 per cent to our understanding of the communication; the rest we take in visually and with our other senses.

As Jonathan Swift wrote in *The Journal of a Modern Lady* in 1729:

> *Nor do they trust their tongue alone,*
> *But speak a language of their own;*
> *Can a nod, a shrug, a look,*
> *Far better than a printed book;*
> *Convey as libel in a frown,*
> *And wink a reputation down.*

It seems that we may give more clues than we perhaps would like to with body language. There is a maxim among massage and beauty therapists: 'The body seldom lies'. When a speaker believes in what they are saying, their whole body language works with them to convey that message powerfully.

Reading the audience's body language

Body language also gives the speaker a good understanding of their audience's attention, response, boredom or aggravation.

When your audience are listening they may tilt their heads, give you lots of eye contact, nod, or increase their blink rate. These signs show that your audience is paying attention to what you have to say. If they are responding positively to your message they may lean forward in their chairs slightly, or adapt an open body posture. Signs include an increasing relaxed attitude of their arms and hands rather than these limbs being held tightly to their bodies. If they are bored they may stare into space or have a slumped posture. If they are rejecting your message, they might doodle on a piece of paper or tap their foot. If they are feeling aggressive they may tap their fingers or foot, stare, lean forwards or clench their fists.

Hopefully you will not have to face the latter two reactions, but if you do, keep concentrating on the positive elements in the audience. Afterwards, review your speech and the environment of the situation to see if you can learn something from the experience. You will find more on dealing with difficult audiences in Step 6, Managing Stage Fright (pp. 87–97).

If you would like to read more about body language, Australian author Allan Pease has written a great book on the subject called *Signals: How to Use Body Language for Power, Success, and Love* – it is well worth reading.

Key factors for your body language when presenting

- Stand tall, shoulders relaxed but back, chest open, head held high and feet slightly apart.

- Do not slouch – you cannot breathe properly when bent over and when you cannot breathe properly it affects your speech.
- Do not give off closed body language signals such as hands tightly clasped, clinging to the lectern and downcast eyes. You will be seen as nervous or even untrustworthy.
- Be open – send out signals that say 'I have nothing to hide'. These signals of honesty are communicated by facing your audience squarely, standing with your arms open, showing the palms of your hands and making sure you use lots of eye contact.

Gestures

Since time began we have been talking with our hands as well as our voices. The Greeks choreographed elaborate hand movements into their plays, the Romans trained their orators not only to speak but also to become accomplished gesturers, and Aboriginals and Native Americans long ago used hand signals and gestures to communicate with different tribes.

Research by prominent linguistic experts around the world shows that gestures predate words as a means of human expression in our evolutionary history. It seems we react to gestures very quickly because certain nerve cells in the lower temples of our brains are dedicated exclusively to this work. Brain image studies show that hand gestures actually come before the moment you become conscious of your own thought.

For most people hands and arms give them acute embarrassment once they stand up to speak. Suddenly those hands and arms seem awkward and out of place. Should they let them hang woodenly by their side? Do they clasp their hands in supplication like a singer? Or do they do the typical royal consort pose of hands behind the back?

The best way to manage is to give them licence to 'talk' naturally as you speak. Become aware of your gestures as you are rehearsing your speech. Once you are aware of how you gesture, start rehearsing these movements with your speech. Most people speak with their hands and it looks more natural than trying to find some compromise pose. But remember to be aware as you rehearse that you might have a microphone in front of you on the 'night' of the performance.

Tips for managing gestures

> *If language was given to men to conceal their thoughts, then gesture's purpose was to disclose them.*
>
> JOHN NAPIER

- The aim is to be as natural and spontaneous as possible – as George Bernard Shaw once said: 'I am the most spontaneous speaker in the world because every word, every gesture, and every retort has been carefully researched.'
- Avoid fake or overly theatrical gestures that can make you look like an enthusiastic traffic cop or an out-of-work star from one of the television soaps.
- A mobile face, that is able to convey humour, sadness, indignation, questioning, is very attractive to the audience and certainly punctuates the spoken word.
- Part of the visual package as a speaker is a smile. A small number of people find it easy to do the immediate smile – all they seem to do is lift the upper lip to show the teeth, open wide and they have a smile. For those who find the 'on-call' Colgate smile a challenge, practise in front of the mirror until you get the smiley face that you like and, most importantly, the one that feels comfortable.

    According to research there are three types of smile: the closed smile, in which the mouth corners are drawn up and out while the teeth remain covered; the upper smile, in which the corners of the mouth are drawn up and out, and the upper lip is raised, revealing some of the upper teeth while the lower teeth remain covered; the broad smile, similar to the upper smile, but with both the upper and lower teeth exposed. So take your pick – closed, upper or broad – I am sure you can drum up a funny or amusing moment to provide sufficient impetus to move those face muscles.

If you are not naturally in tune with your inner feelings, it will take courage and effort to find your 'inner voice'. I encourage you to work at finding this, whether you define your inner voice as your soul, your life force or the authentic you. It is this honesty that will take you from being a competent speaker to a good, if not great speaker.

When you are true to yourself in your language, gestures and appearance, you will powerfully connect with your audience. When you really 'do it your way' a magical, almost mystical alliance happens with your audience. It is this palpable feeling of oneness that creates lasting memories of that sweet moment of true achievement.

STEP 5

HOW TO SPEAK POWERFULLY

When I dare to be powerful, to use my strength in the service of my vision, then it becomes less and less important whether I am afraid.

AUDRE LORDE, *American writer, activist and educator, 1934–92*

Find out why you need to use plain English, how to bring your speech to life with texture and pause, and why rehearsing your speech will give you confidence.

Speak simply and succinctly

I don't let my mouth say nothing my head can't stand.

LOUIS ARMSTRONG

The best speakers use language that is easily understood by their audience. They do not put their listeners under pressure trying to piece together what they are saying. Conversely, speakers who determinedly use language grander than their audience's ability to understand, will alienate their listeners. Such speakers are often trying to impress or may be professionals or academics who thoughtlessly use their everyday 'speak'. They do not take into account the audience's lack of knowledge of their chosen language or subject. Relevance to the audience's level of comprehension is paramount for any speaker. If you want them to listen to what you have to say, you must put your message into words that the majority can understand.

Our language is constantly evolving. Our dictionaries are growing richer and fatter with every new edition. New words and phrases are taking over from the old. In his book *Mother Tongue*, Bill Bryson reports that Robert Birchfield, editor of the *Oxford English Dictionary*, believes that 'American English and English English are drifting apart so remorselessly that one day the two nations may not be able to understand each other at all'.

From this it is not too difficult to see that we have areas in communication that are not straightforward. For instance, if you are speaking to an older audience or if you are an older person speaking to a younger market, you could have a generation language gap. How we spoke four or even two decades ago will have subtle differences from today's modern language. Yesterday we were more formal in our speech; today we talk in a more relaxed manner. If you are speaking to a group of baby boomers or a group of teenagers your choice of words and phrases should complement their lifetime frame of understanding. Consider the difference in choice of words to ask the same question:

Yesterday: Is that convenient or suitable for you?
Today: Is that cool?
Yesterday: I love your new dress.
Today: Way cool threads, man.

Relevance to the audience must always be the speaker's highest priority. If you gloss over this, you run the risk of alienating your audience.

I am sure you have experienced speakers who appear arrogant and puffed up with a sense of their own self-importance. They seem insensitive to their audience, using words and phrases that are out of reach of the understanding of the average listener. They drone on relentlessly, apparently oblivious to any discomfort their listeners might feel.

It may be that a few of these speakers are naturally arrogant. This, as Benjamin Disraeli so aptly put it, is the 'sophisticated rhetorician, inebriated with the exuberance of their own verbosity'. Unfortunately they believe that if the audience doesn't understand, then that is the audience's loss.

But not all pretentious speakers fall into that category. For some novice or anxious speakers, language provides the temptation to promote themselves as something other than they are. They believe their words just don't seem important enough to make their audience sit up and take notice. They search for the perfect word – their own will not do. In a desire to project a smarter intellectual element into their speech they turn to the dictionary or thesaurus to 'borrow' the ideal word or phrase, believing that someone else would definitely be able to put it better than they would. To them this equates with greater audience approval.

There is absolutely nothing wrong with using a dictionary or thesaurus to look for a new way to say something. On the contrary, the richness of the English language offers us an abundance of synonyms that will give depth of shade and light to whatever you want to express. But you must know and be comfortable using these words. This is an important point for new or anxious speakers to grasp – always use language that you are familiar with. You do not need obstacle words looming in your speech for you to somehow scramble over – your language must be easily in your grasp.

Let's look at some examples:

She is a chiromancer.
She reads palms.

> *Always use language that you are familiar with.*

It is obvious he is a polymath.
Clearly, he has extensive knowledge about many subjects.

The cappuccino at this café is incredibly spumescent.
The cappuccino at this café is incredibly frothy.

Most members of the audience will not know what a 'chiromancer' or a 'polymath' are and they will spend valuable moments trying to decipher or to retain the words for future reference. More people may understand 'spumescent' but because it is an interestingly different word they might focus on the word unnecessarily, thus interrupting the flow of their listening.

The important lesson here is to remember that by using unnecessarily pretentious language, you actually diminish the impact of your message. So don't be a word chaser; put your message into your own style of speech and language and say it with conviction. If your everyday language fits into the 'high-brow' category, you need to consider your audience's capacity to understand what you are saying. If you are not addressing like-minded peers, simplify your language into plain English so that everyone can understand the value of your talk.

CELEBRITY TIP

Use language with which you are comfortable. If you need to pronounce any unusual names, make sure you know how to do so correctly. If there are other words you're not sure how to pronounce, don't use them! Vary the length of your sentences. It can be effective to use some very, very short sentences in among longer ones. And sometimes, it is okay to break the rules of grammar for effect (as I just have), by beginning a sentence with 'and' or 'but'. But know why you are doing it – for dramatic effect.

Don't be self-indulgent. You are there for what you can bring to the audience. Speak in terms both you – and they – can easily understand. Remember, it is harder to absorb the spoken word than the written word.

LYNDEY MILAN

Jargon is another honeybee trap for the insecure or pretentious speaker. Jargon, argot or shoptalk that is used widely in the workplace has now crept into people's everyday language. Every occupation, sport or hobby has words and expressions that are special to that group. Lots of speakers love to hide behind jargon. It defines their status and gives them a sense of value in being a member of a unique group of people, which is great for work, sport or hobby activities where everyone understands the language. But if that language is outside the audience's experience and understanding, it can be interpreted as elitist and rude. There is always a risk when jargon is used that the audience may not understand or appreciate it. 'Please explain' is not how you want to leave your audience feeling.

Would you ever say something like: 'We interfaced with the objective of continuing the dialogue'? I have heard much more tortured phrases surfacing in industry seminars and even more sadly used by conference speakers when speaking to a lay audience.

How to avoid being pretentious

- Find out in detail the make-up of the audience and always speak to that level.
- If it is a lay audience remember to de-clutter any jargon and demystify your prose. If it is a professional audience of your peers, this is a different matter but your language should primarily target the needs of your audience.
- Avoid using unfamiliar, convoluted words when simpler ones would be more effective.
- Shorten sentences if they seem too long. The audience will find short sentences easier to understand. It is also easier for you to take a breath while speaking.
- Try to avoid jargon, even if you pepper your working life with it. Jargon is the quickest way to lose your lay audience. It is exclusive and offensive to the uninitiated listener. Too much jargon will even make an industry-aware audience switch off as it can be boring for those who hear it every day. It is also possible that your jargon may have subtle differences from theirs.
- Use titles in full rather than unfamiliar acronyms that are part of our working language. While it is fine to use the acronym in your industry sector, this is an absolute no-no if you are not sure your audience will be able to interpret it.
- Use memory prompter speech notes with key headings for each topic or idea (see pp. 52–53). They are a great way to counteract any inflated word use. By using key words only, you soon lose any words that you may have 'borrowed', forcing you back into your more natural way of speaking.

Add texture to your speech

*Words mean more than what is set down on paper.
It takes the human voice to infuse them with the shades
of deeper meaning.*

MAYA ANGELOU, *I Know Why the Caged Bird Sings*

When developing a recipe a good cook will always consider the flavour and texture of the dish. A dish with the added dimension of texture is more interesting to the palate. It is the same with the delivery of a speech. Texture gives the listener additional listening excitement. While the cook looks for ingredients that will be compatible with the flavours of the dish, the public speaker can inject texture with variations in tone, pace, volume, facial movements, gestures and the all-important pause.

His speech flowed from his tongue sweeter than honey.

HOMER, *The Iliad*

Think back to some of the speeches you have experienced as a listener. You have probably heard quite a few, from the boring management talk to the brilliant motivational speaker, from the nervous, stumbling speaker at a recent sports club meeting to the funny and happy twenty-first birthday speech.

I am sure the ones that have really struck home have been the speeches that were delivered with enthusiasm. Enthusiasm is infectious. Laughter is infectious; catching it is easy. After a moment of watching, your smile starts to beam and the laugh comes bubbling up. Enthusiasm does the same thing. It reaches out to the heart of the listener and they are carried along with the eager flow. Enthusiasm will drive the texture, pace and volume of your speech. It will pepper it with energy. It will carry you across the waters of your words with grace and charm.

Where do you find enthusiasm? It is your speech – your hard-earned thoughts and views, your well-crafted words, you own the speech, you are proud of it – so let it show.

> **CELEBRITY TIP**
>
> Be enthusiastic, for there is nothing more engaging than genuine enthusiasm. Have fun. Remember how scary it can be on a roller-coaster, yet once you get off you want to do it all over again. A speech can be like that, so enjoy the ride the first time!
>
> LYNDEY MILAN

Tone

In a recent television documentary about a master class for opera singers, some established opera stars with many years of singing experience behind them, were being coached in how to paint the emotions of the story of the opera with their voices. The maestro was cajoling, pleading and berating each singer until he could hear the right level of humility, joy, sadness or drama in the aria. As they progressed you could feel only too well the difference from the initial delivery. Suddenly the music and libretto were transformed; a new dimension of energy and passion had been achieved.

When speaking to an audience we need to aim to achieve that extra dimension, that life force that comes from using our voice to paint a picture. Our tone of voice is one of the tools we have to create the layers of richness and character of our speech.

Pace

The optimum pace of speaking depends a lot on the normal speaking pace of the speaker. Some speakers just plain dawdle and the audience is almost on its toes waiting for the next word to drop. Other speakers think it is a race and go at breakneck speed with the audience hanging on for dear life trying to comprehend. Both paces are frustrating and a turn-off for the audience.

You should aim for about 140–160 words a minute. You probably will not know how fast or slow that pace is unless you have taped yourself and counted every word in the sixty seconds. So let's say a moderate pace – neither breakneck nor snail's pace.

The human ear is capable of deciphering up to 400 words per minute. So you can see that if your pace is too slow the audience's minds will wander. Determining the pace is a little like the story of 'Goldilocks and the Three Bears'. Papa and Mama Bear can be discounted because they are too extreme, but Baby Bear's pace is just right. Listen to the pace of other speakers or ask your friends to evaluate your pace of delivery to find your own Baby Bear pace.

Volume

I am sure you have been to meetings or events where you have been frustrated by not being able to hear the speaker properly. If you want to kill communication, this is the way to do it. If the audience cannot hear you, they will switch off. As a conference organiser I am always amazed that some people do not take into account the need to invest in some good audio equipment, or to have an audio engineer present throughout the speaking program, or if it is a small meeting and there is no microphone, that the speaker does not understand the need to project their voice sufficiently to be heard.

You must take this into account when you are speaking at any event. If you are speaking at a venue where there is a microphone make sure that you use it correctly (see Using different microphones, pp. 128–132.) If there is no microphone you must work out how far you need to project your voice (see p. 80). It makes me sad and frustrated that speakers put so much effort into preparing a presentation only to have all this talent, time and energy wasted if the audience cannot hear them properly.

It does not happen just to inexperienced people. I recently attended two meetings that promised to deliver a high level of excitement and motivation. The speakers had been carefully selected to leave the audience begging for more. It was obvious from the front rows and the speakers' body inflections and smiles that this is what they were giving those lucky people. Unfortunately for the rest of us towards the back of the venue, we only caught one word in ten as the speaker raised their voice to punctuate what they were saying. Some of those at the back who had better hearing were concentrating so intently that they were finding it hard to take notes. Although we kept giving the message both verbally and physically by cupping our ears that we could not hear, astonishingly it fell on 'deaf ears' and the level of volume from the microphone did not increase.

Please don't waste your time and talents by not checking or investigating the volume you need to achieve. Don't be reticent in asking to test the microphone.

USING TONE, PACE AND VOLUME EFFECTIVELY

- Use enthusiasm to put a palpable buzz into your presentation.
- There is nothing as flat, or such a turn-off to the audience as delivering your speech in a monotone. Even the word 'monotone' sounds lifeless and bland. You need to punctuate, to paint your words with passion. If you know you speak in a monotone, use techniques such as tonal and pace variety to build or decrease the tension or to highlight key points of your speech.

- A common Australian habit is the rising inflection, where the voice rises, often rather squeakily, at the end of a sentence, so that it sounds as though we are posing a question rather than making a statement. This is not an endearing national trait. Avoid rising inflection like you would body odour. Like body odour you may sometimes be unaware that it is your problem. Ask a friend to tell you whether or not you do use a rising inflection and, if you have this habit, do something about overcoming it.

- Listen to other speakers, become aware of their pace of speaking. When you find the pace you enjoy listening to, model your pace on this.

- You can effectively use pace to highlight elements of your speech. Reduce or increase the pace in key parts of the speech to improve the sense of the material. When you rehearse, mark your notes with asterisks to denote a change in pace. A well-constructed speech will have a rhythm of its own and it is only by speaking the piece that you will know how to colour and punctuate with the pace of your voice.

- If you are using a microphone, talk in your normal speaking voice. If you have a very soft voice you may need to project your voice slightly, even with the microphone. Make sure that the microphone is checked for volume beforehand. Make sure you know how to use it correctly (see pp. 128–132).

- If you are at a public meeting where there is no microphone you will need to project your voice so that everyone can hear you. Make sure you stand to speak, as this will help your ability to project your voice. Don't shout, but speak loudly and visualise projecting or pushing your voice to the far end of the room. Practise projecting your voice at home or at another suitable place. As you speak, envision your voice reaching the far corners of the room.

The pause

As the late great actor Sir Ralph Richardson said: 'The most precious things in speech are pauses'. A pause will fill the 'void'; it will capture attention and will punctuate, illuminate and build the tension in a speech.

Do you remember sitting in class at school, your mind skimming over the teacher's voice as if you were anywhere but there, when suddenly the teacher stops and there is a great wide yawning pause. By its very silence you immediately come back to the present moment.

A pause is also a very useful tool in speech-making; it certainly works well to bring back an audience that has 'gone off the boil'. It can also be used most effectively to capture and instil that tense moment of expectation. Comedians use the pause well – the secret is all in the timing of the delivery. They also use pace and tonal variety to give a tempo to their lines. Start observing comedians and see how timing and the pause can really deliver a joke.

A pause should be just that – not a creeping period of silence, but a moment when talking ceases and you are aware that the audience is waiting on the impact of your next statement. When do you use the pause? You can use it to emphasise a key idea or the thesis of the speech, to deliver punchlines in a humorous speech, to change the pace or direction of your speech, and to bring your speech to a conclusion.

Rehearse your speech

It isn't what I do, but how I do it. It isn't what I say but how I say it – and how I look when I do and say it.

MAE WEST

You have your speech together, you've prepared your speech notes. You have reviewed it closely to see if it would benefit from additional texture from pace, tone or the pause and you have marked any verbal punctuations on your notes with an asterisk. Now you need to find a quiet spot to practise. Ideally it is a space where you can lock yourself away from interruptions and disturbances and has a good size or full-length mirror. I find my bathroom best as there is a large mirror which enables me to see my facial expressions and gestures and the room is quiet and sufficiently away from the main activity areas in my home to be quiet. Most importantly, that mirror reminds me to pull my shoulders down and back so that my posture looks and feels good.

As you rehearse within the comfort of your home surroundings, you will notice your timing will be fairly consistent. However, when you actually deliver the speech in front of a live audience you will find it takes longer. As you connect with the audience your pace and content of delivery may be affected. You may add a comment or two, or you may just slow the pace a fraction to accommodate audience reaction. So always leave room in your speech for it to expand slightly.

I have seen and known many speakers who leave the preparation of important speaking assignments to the last moment and who obviously have not rehearsed or timed their presentation but come along with their notes in hand, hoping for the best. Frequently these people go horribly over time, some even being asked to finish long before they have completed their material. This is not only humiliating for the speaker, irritating to the audience and an organiser's nightmare, it affects the rest of the programming as the organiser desperately tries to borrow time from tea and meal breaks or even worse from other speakers' question time. You need to start good habits right from the start of your speaking career.

CELEBRITY TIP

Before your presentation, rehearse – out loud. This is a vital part of any preparation. I can recall many cases where 'first-time' speakers have been startled by the sound of their own voice, especially if they are using a microphone. Ask someone whose judgement you trust to listen, and offer an opinion about pace, inflection, phrasing and so on.

IAN ROSS

Key factors when rehearsing

- Put your heart into the rehearsal; practise your facial movements, tone and pace variety and gestures. Reach the stage where you are totally comfortable with all of these things. If you find the odd sentence still does not sit well, rework it until it fits.
- How many times you rehearse is up to you. It is said that Winston Churchill would rehearse for anything up to eight hours for a forty-minute speech. It is a question of finding the right balance for your needs. If you are a relatively new speaker I suggest you rehearse your speech over and over and over, or until you feel absolutely comfortable and confident with every word and action. This may well take you some time until your confidence peaks and you have the speech as you want it.
- Obviously the more experienced you are as a speaker, the less practice runs you will need. However, even the most experienced orator needs time to run though any presentation to achieve a successful outcome.
- Go through your speech twice with an eye to the timing. Edit it again if necessary to meet the specified time. Then continue rehearsing and timing your speech. Always aim to come well under time when rehearsing at home.

- New research by British neuroscientist, Baroness Susan Greenfield, shows that visualising an activity can be as beneficial as actually doing it. Obviously this makes any repetitive rehearsal of your speech more convenient as you can alternate between speaking out loud and quietly sitting in a relaxed state while visualising every nuance, gesture and progress of the speech.
- Practise your stage fright management techniques (see pp. 91–96).

Speaking to time

I cannot stress enough that speaking to the allotted time is vital. This is because:

- The organisers' agenda or program takes into account the timing of other speakers' presentations, the catering breaks and most importantly the audience's limits and needs. When you go overtime, time has to be garnered from somewhere and invariably it will affect the overall running and enjoyment of the event.

Speaking to the allotted time is vital.

- Audiences have zero tolerance of speakers who go over time.
- Undisciplined speakers, however talented and valuable their presentation, do themselves a big disservice. Invariably they are not asked to speak again as people consider them too much of a risk.
- If you aim to speak professionally you must lay down good habits in the early stages of your speaking career.

Podiums, lecterns, tables or just you

A podium is a small raised platform of indiscriminate height that provides sufficient height for an elevation over the seated audience. When getting up to speak, be aware of how you reach and step up to the podium. There may be steps to ascend or it may be low enough for you to step onto. Always give yourself that extra edge of preparation by arriving early to see the venue and how you are going to access this platform. Be grateful for the podium as it gives you that power advantage of being above your audience.

A lectern is defined as a reading desk but think of it as sufficiently tall and small-faced to hold your papers as you speak. Lecterns come in all shapes and sizes from the tubular 'music stand' variety to the heavy ornate wooden job. Be thankful for the lectern as it does provide a minuscule hide that is very comforting for the newer speaker. It enables you to rest your speaker's notes easily and has room to move them unobtrusively to the side as you speak. If the lectern's height can be changed, make sure it is the right level for you. If the lectern height cannot be altered, make sure that the audience can see you clearly from mid-chest up. If it is too tall for you then it is better to stand by the side of the lectern where you can still place your notes on one side of the lectern sill.

It may be that you are at a meeting where there is no podium or lectern and the only barrier between you and the audience is a trestle table. Always stand up to speak. Hold your speaker's notes in your hand and as you complete each memory prompter, slide it behind the others.

Memory prompter speech notes (see pp. 52–53) are always easier to handle than A4 sheets of copy. If you are frightened that the audience will see the notes shaking in your hands, use the notes to gesture; that will help you overcome that nervous energy. If the 'dreaded shakes' (a common fear for most speakers) do surface, keep refocusing on what you are saying and allow those hands to express themselves.

> **CELEBRITY TIP**
>
> *Never read a speech.* It's vitally important to know *what* you're going to say … highlighting key words and glancing down to keep on track is acceptable. Put the required hours in, go over and over it, remember what you're saying and deliver your speech as if it's just coming into your head for the first time.
>
> If you're delivering a written speech, be sure to use a larger font and wide spacing between lines, highlighting important words or thoughts. I like to use a size 16 font in Arial with one and a half line spaces in between. It helps to keep your place when you quickly glance down.
>
> DEBORAH HUTTON

When you try to be something you're not, the people in your audience will see through it. A few people might be impressed if you use borrowed language or language that does not appropriately address the level of the audience's understanding, but this would be a hollow victory. To reach the widest audience, use language that sits well with you, words that comfortably roll off the tongue. Avoid jargon and acronyms. Use pace, volume and pauses to texture your speech. Remember to find a moderate pace that allows the audience to absorb the words. Too fast and you have left them at the post; too slow and they will lose interest. A judicious pause will always bring the audience back into the 'now'. When you rehearse, take into account the timing of your speech. Always bring it in slightly under time, as it frequently takes longer to deliver a speech in front of a live audience. A full-length mirror is your best friend when you first start to rehearse as it enables you to understand clearly what your audience will see. Intersperse rehearsing out loud with quietly sitting and visualising every word and movement until you are conscious that your language and gestures come together effortlessly and confidently.

MANAGING STAGE FRIGHT

You can conquer almost any fear if you will make up your mind to do so. For remember fear doesn't exist except in the mind.

DALE CARNEGIE, *American lecturer, author and pioneer in the field of public speaking and the psychology of the successful personality*

Find out why we suffer from performance anxiety and how to develop strategies to cope with it.

'Well and good,' I can hear you say. 'I have reached this stage, I have worked hard on overcoming my fears and insecurity issues, I have found my authentic voice and am ready to speak. But the one big thing you have not told me is how to deal with stage fright.'

For the vast majority of speakers, stage fright presents itself in all-consuming reality. The butterflies don't flutter in the pit of your stomach; they play touch football. Your chest is tight and you are obsessed with the loud thump-thump of your heart that drums in your ears. Your mouth becomes so dry that it causes your top lip to hook unattractively on your front upper teeth.

Then comes the absolute, sheer crippling terror that grips you as the time for you to speak draws closer. Will you be able to walk to the stage, or stand at the lectern if you reach it? You know without a doubt that all the practice in the world will not help you now. You are convinced you will barely be able to speak, that you won't remember a word. You are so deep within the grip of these fears that your body is rigid or shakes.

> ## CELEBRITY TIP
>
> No situation, audience or external factor can actually make you nervous. Whenever you feel nerves creeping on, simply remind yourself: 'This is me making myself nervous – let's chill out a bit here – I'm really not making it any easier for myself'. Then remember the last time you were shit-scared about something but pulled through. You'll be fine.
>
> ADAM SPENCER

When you are feeling stage fright you are experiencing the 'fright or flight' syndrome. This was very common to our early ancestors as they hunted wild beasts. When you are frightened, the adrenal glands secrete adrenaline into the bloodstream. In this state blood is sent to the major muscles and organs, which provides the muscles with more energy reserves to call on. Very useful when you are about to kill a mammoth with a spear for supper but quite debilitating when the symptoms have no real physical action to release them.

Stage fright or performance nerves or anxiety is very real. Whether the anxieties are specific or a collection of terrors is not important. Surveys of speakers have identified some common fears:

- Some speakers are afraid the audience will judge them critically.
- Some think they will lose the plot entirely when they reach the lectern and not be able to speak or remember what their speech is about.
- Others consider the content of their speech is not good enough.

For most of us stage fright is a fact of life. Many performers do not like owning up to performance nerves but it is hypothesised that about 95 per cent of performers suffer from stage fright. Some who have disclosed this include Barbra Streisand, James Garner, Sir Winston Churchill and Sir Laurence Olivier. Lord Olivier suffered so badly from stage fright that he commented: 'Stage fright is always waiting outside the door, waiting to get you. You either battle it or walk away'. Walking away was not an option for him and, hopefully, after reading this chapter, it won't be for you either.

The good side of this nerve-racking experience is that these nerves and the subsequent adrenalin release provide you with the dynamics to perform with more vitality and energy than you ever imagined. If you understand that performance nerves are beneficial, even though they feel decidedly wretched at the time, you are on track to accepting that they are a useful phase in the lead-up to performing successfully on stage.

As they are part and parcel of performing for the majority of us, the trick lies in managing these symptoms rather than allowing them to take control. First, let's look at what a big surge of adrenaline may do to your body.

- It increases your heart rate.
- Your breathing becomes more rapid.
- Time is distorted – everything seems to happen in slow motion.
- You feel detached from reality.
- The pupils of your eyes dilate.
- Your hair might stand on end.

- You have a dry mouth.
- Your voice quivers.
- Your body shakes.
- You find you are sweating, your palms and forehead are damp.
- You may have a feeling of nausea.
- You may feel the need to run to the toilet.
- You may feel that you are frozen to the spot.

For the first five years of my speaking career I suffered excessively from stage fright. Not only did I endure debilitating performance nerves but I also saw this as failure on my part and emotionally threw in the towel during the speech which, of course, meant that I sabotaged any efforts to reach my full potential.

My watershed came when I was driving to compete in another speech contest. Yet again, I was manifesting feelings of anxiety and failure. I decided then and there that it was sheer lunacy to keep doing this to myself. If I could not find some way to manage the effects of stage fright and be able to enjoy giving a speech then I would give it away.

I accepted that this was make or break time and I was committed to entering this particular speech contest. I decided to take the pressure off myself by trying an alternative way of tackling the problem. A couple of weeks earlier I had read an article about creative visualisation or imaging. So, primed with a little knowledge, I spent the rest of my journey to the venue simply focusing on seeing myself having fun at the lectern and the audience smiling back at me and obviously enjoying my presentation.

Amazingly, when I arrived, I felt more relaxed than I had ever done before and able to cope with the residual nervous symptoms. As I waited to speak I still determinedly focused on a positive outcome of enjoyment and pleasure, pushing away any niggling doubts about my performance that still tried to take over. When I was introduced, I walked confidently to the lectern, and the delivery of the speech was as I had visualised: I enjoyed each word, phrase and gesture and the audience loved the speech. More importantly, I broke the drought, not only beating the gremlins but winning the contest! I still experience stage fright in varying degrees depending on the occasion but I know it is something that I can manage, providing I do my preparation beforehand.

CELEBRITY TIP

I am almost always nervous about going on stage, but I find the nervous energy is a very important part of what fuels the energy of my performance. If I don't have some kind of butterflies before a performance I find that the show will generally be a disaster. I don't want to manage my stage fright. That energy is an important part of what I have to give to the audience. I was a cast member of the *Vagina Monologues* and the director talked about imagining all the anxiety, nervous thoughts and anticipation moving freely throughout the body. She said: 'Don't repress the energy. When you step out onto the stage, imagine all that energy flowing out in front of you filling the stage and hall. The energy is what makes a performance electric.' I have to agree.

TONI CHILDS

Managing symptoms of stage fright

First you need to accept that stage fright or nerves are part and parcel of your body physiologically readying itself to stand alone and be accountable in the spotlight. Once you understand how your body responds, the fear is more manageable each time you speak. You know that you have been there before and survived.

Recognise that these symptoms of nerves are less discernible to an audience than you imagine and that when you do reach the lectern and actually speak those fears fade away and amazingly you are back in control within a very short time. As David J. Schwartz states in his book *The Magic of Thinking Big*, 'action cures fear'. It is estimated that for most people these pre-lectern physiological symptoms last roughly ten minutes. It probably seems longer because one of the symptoms of 'fright and flight' is time distortion – everything seems a little slower.

We need to have some techniques to make this nervous energy work for us, not against us. There are band-aid exercises that will definitely ease some of the symptoms at the event. But if you are suffused by these terrors immediately prior to your performance, you will find it very hard to put these into practice, which is why I encourage you to start stage fright management techniques well in advance of speaking so you are fully prepared.

Most of us have an inner terrorist who lurks about in our conscious and subconscious minds, determined to tell us that we are inadequate, not capable, don't have the ability, and so on. This terrorist is so good at the job and his or her strikes are so constant that we are not even aware how many times a day he or she scores a direct hit – so we accept the negative message completely. Imagine the belief drain you will experience if you partner this with performance nerves.

Meditation techniques

Meditation is acknowledged as one of the best things you can do for your mind, body and spirit. Meditation quietens the mind so that you can reprogram your subconscious and conscious minds with positive self-images. If you have not practised meditation before, why not investigate the many different meditation styles available through classes or workshops. You can also purchase quality tapes and CDs which teach you to meditate. There are literally hundreds of meditation methods so choose one that suits you. Make the intention of your meditation to focus on positive-self messages or affirmations.

Even if you are not into meditation, you should find the following variety of simple techniques that fall broadly under the banner of meditative practice helpful.

REPROGRAMMING

Randy Gage is one of the world's leading motivational speakers. His simple method for reprogramming the subconscious mind is this: sit upright in a chair with your arms resting on the chair or in your lap. Relax. Keep the palms of your hands upwards. Breathe in deeply through the nose and gently release the breath through your mouth. With each breath, count from fifty downwards. Concentrate on a steady rhythmic breathing. If at first your mind washes up all the should-do, would-do issues of everyday life, let these thoughts flow over you and gently pull your mind back to breathing in and out. When you reach zero, acknowledge mentally that 'I am in an alpha state'.

Our brains give off electrical activity which is displayed in the form of brainwaves. These brainwaves include beta waves, when the mind is strongly engaged, theta waves when we are in 'day-dreaming' mode and finally delta waves when we are asleep. But it is the alpha brainwave state that is important for absorbing positive self-messages and reprogramming. The alpha state is the very relaxed and meditative phase of brainwave activity, often experienced just before you go to sleep. It is a very dreamy and pleasant state. You can experience this in meditation by taking time out to reflect in a quiet natural setting – such as a walk in a garden, sitting quietly watching the ocean, or watching clouds scud by.

When you are in this alpha state, then start reprogramming with positive affirmations. These might include statements such as 'I am a valuable person', 'My audience love me', 'I am a dynamic speaker', 'I believe in myself'. As you repeat your affirmations several times, feel it, believe it. When you have finished count down slowly from five to one and mentally acknowledge that you will wake refreshed and renewed. Should you nod off before reaching zero, shorten the number of breaths to accommodate this. As you practise more frequently bring the count up to fifty again.

ANCHORING

In Neuro-Linguistic Programming, an 'anchor' (an NLP tool) is 'any stimulus that changes your state'. The stimulus can be different triggers, for example, the recollection of music, a smell or a picture.

While presenting, use the anchor to strongly recall a moment of personal achievement and as this memory positively imprints in your mind ground this feeling by giving yourself a tactile signal by pressing the thumb and third finger together. When you first start using this technique you will need to practise recalling a happy and satisfactory experience at will and as the memory surfaces anchor it by pressing your thumb and third finger together. It is good to do this when you are in a pleasant, relaxed alpha state. This tactile signal can then be used in challenging or difficult moments to centre you and your thoughts.

I discovered that I had been using this type of practice long before I read about NLP, as I found that a touch or gentle pressure helped me to reassure myself.

MEDITATIVE RELAXATION

As you first focus on breathing rhythmically, change your focus onto consciously relaxing a specific part of your body, say, your left hand. As you relax your hand identify clearly how this feeling of relaxation affects your breathing and your mind. Practise this many times until you are able to get in touch quickly with the feeling that relaxation gives you. Combine this with the 'anchor' technique of recalling the relaxed feeling by pressing the thumb and third finger together for the most effective results.

CALMING DEEP BREATHING

Deep breathing exercises are excellent because they allow you to focus not only on the breath but on the rhythm of the breath. Breathe in through the nose, silently count 'one', and breathe out through the mouth, silently counting 'two, three, four'. Breathe in and out slowly and steadily, focusing on your breathing and counting. This exercise is the perfect antidote for rampant nerves that appear just before that walk to the lectern. (See also Breath management and performance anxiety, p. 117.)

CREATIVE VISUALISATION FOR SUCCESS

Using creative visualisation or imaging to see yourself in a relaxed and happy state as you perform is the most effective method for people who suffer badly from stage fright (see pp. 90–91). Relaxation and deep breathing exercises are very good for helping you to control the fear before speaking but *positive* imaging gives you real ammunition to blow those fears out of the water!

Begin your calming deep breathing and focus on this breathing until you are in a relaxed state. When you are in this relaxed state, paint yourself a picture of you walking confidently to the lectern or wherever you are going to speak. At the lectern, you face the audience squarely, you are relaxed and at ease. See yourself start to speak, the words that are such a part of you now flow freely, you are articulate and convincing. Feel your confidence grow. See how the audience are engrossed, appreciating every word, leaning forward slightly in their chairs. Taste the sense of achievement that you experience as your speech draws to a conclusion. See the audience as they respond enthusiastically to a great presentation.

Repeat this process two or three times. 'Anchor' this feeling of success in your mind.

On the day of the performance

- Find a quiet half-hour to go through your meditative relaxation and creative visualisation for success exercises once more.
- Check you have your notes and plan to arrive with plenty of time to check the venue and sound system before the start of the event.
- If possible, have a look round the venue, see where you will speak and where you will sit. Walk to the stage or area where you will speak. Test the lectern height, if there is one, and the sound system. Decide where you need to place the microphone for your needs. If there is no microphone, determine how far you will need to project your voice.
- If none of this is possible, don't worry. You will be able to observe everything when you have access to the area. Also you or the organiser will be able to change the microphone height, if needed, once you reach the lectern.
- If you begin to feel even remotely nervous or anxious, go into either the meditative relaxation or calming deep breathing exercises and focus on this until you have those gremlins under control.
- If you are eating beforehand, eat lightly as you could feel uncomfortable if you eat too much. Avoid alcohol, coffee or tea, as alcohol and caffeine combined with a hearty injection of adrenaline will have you climbing the walls. Stick to water until after the speech.
- After eating, check your teeth for any food; check you are comfortable with the rest of your appearance.
- Drink lots of lukewarm or tepid water, it is kinder on the voice – avoid iced water as the difference in temperature

range between the larynx and the iced water is too great, no matter what the outside temperature. If you are in a public meeting take a bottle of water with you, and remember to keep it at room temperature.

- Only if it is possible and you can find somewhere private, do some voice and facial exercises to warm up. If not, make sure you do a good couple of deep yawns before speaking. (For more information, see Tongue twisters to tease and please, pp. 118–120 and Other warm-up exercises, p. 120.)
- Again, if you start to feel anxious at any stage, use one of your anchoring techniques and focus on your deep breathing.
- Make a cognitive shift in your thinking – push away quickly from any self-limiting thoughts.
- Keep focused on presenting a rewarding and fulfilling speech.

CELEBRITY TIP

I've always suffered from stage fright. However, it became debilitating when I was working in magazine publishing and was at times required to be interviewed for television. I couldn't think straight and delivered nonsense answers that just made me look foolish. From then I made a vow to myself that if I was given the opportunity to have another crack at it, I'd pull it off. The rest is history. Overcoming the stage fright was a purely mental thing and simply required focus. I would channel all of my attention to the words rather than thinking beyond my immediate environment. And I would literally block out the people around me. It requires a kind of discipline and, of course, being prepared is a must. Doing some yoga has helped and deep breathing is very relaxing. However, not taking it too seriously is the real key – it's supposed to be fun!

SHANNON FRICKE

STEP 7

CONNECTING WITH THE AUDIENCE

Words are, of course, the most powerful drug used by mankind.

RUDYARD KIPLING, *novelist and poet, 1865–1936*

Use eye contact for positive approbation. Find out how to deal with a difficult or hostile audience and how to manage question time.

Finally the time comes when everything you have been working towards is suddenly upon you. The moment is here; you are as ready as you will ever be when your cue comes. You have rehearsed your performance until it rings in your ears. You have practised your stage fright management techniques and the nerves are reasonably under control as you rise to your feet, walk confidently to the lectern and face your moment of self-discovery.

There, in front of you, are row after row of people sitting quietly with impenetrable gazes, waiting expectantly for you to speak. Your first words tumble out nervously but as you progress through the familiar territory of your speech you start to see a positive response from your audience.

Communication is a two-way process. Like you, the audience are hoping that you feel confident and will deliver a satisfying speech. They want you to make them feel you are in control of the situation. The more confident and relaxed you are, the more relaxed they become and their level of enjoyment or interest increases. As you become aware of this support and interest, your confidence grows. You are in control of this collection of words that you have so carefully crafted and rehearsed. Your speech comes to life and the audience's level of response increases. One feeds off the other.

Occasionally, with a good audience and the delivery of a quality speech, you become so in tune with this group of people that you achieve a platinum moment of feeling as one with the audience. This feeling of unity is unbelievably satisfying. It is almost as if you were conducting a magnificent orchestra who are enthusiastically hanging on the next wave from the baton so that they can show their willingness by responding instantly and hungrily for the next sentence.

For most of us public speaking is an enormous step in personal development. It means that you have had to work at managing emotions that are self-defeating. You have developed the courage to speak out and have spent time and effort finding the right words to be a vehicle for your ideas. You have done the preparation; now is the time to communicate your message to your audience in an intimate way.

Make eye contact

The eyes of men converse as much as their tongues,
with the advantage that the ocular dialect needs no

dictionary, but is understood all the world over.

RALPH WALDO EMERSON, *The Conduct of Life*

You create this intimacy with members of the audience through eye contact.

Ever since the advent of silent movies, film producers have focused on the chemistry of eyes meeting across crowded rooms, empty landscapes and a million other settings. Think of the thousands of meaningful looks that have been used on the big screen to inject sensuality or drama onto the celluloid.

Leonardo da Vinci's *Mona Lisa* is probably the most famous painting to come out of the Renaissance period. It is a painting that has intrigued the world over the centuries with its portrait of an unknown model, sombrely dressed, gazing piercingly out at us with eyes that seem to follow us wherever we go. We are bewitched, entranced and captivated by those eyes.

In Western culture eye contact expresses confidence and communicates trust and integrity. In cultures where there is an absence of eye contact it may indicate deference to those more powerful. On our TV sets each day we meet the strong, uninterrupted gaze of newsreaders and identities as they speak, it would seem, directly to us. We see these people, who are not afraid to look us in the eye as they speak, as more trustworthy and appealing.

We cannot deny the language of our eyes. Our words may express the opposite but our eyes will always tell the truth. As Ralph Waldo Emerson went on to say in *The Conduct of Life*, 'When the eyes say one thing, and the tongue another, a practiced man relies on the language of the first'.

Eye contact allows you to monitor the impact of your words upon the audience. Without eye contact your pace tends to speed up and your speech lacks vitality. The energy you get from positive eye contact will psyche you up. It is a sure-fire way to experience assurance and warmth. These feelings of acceptance will linger long after your speech has concluded. If you are doing your job with courage you will find many 'pairs of sparkling eyes meeting yours across a crowded room'. The buzz from this is palpable – it raises your game and increases your confidence.

As a member of any future audience you will now think differently about the importance of your role as a listener.

It is said that the eyes are the windows of the soul and as a speaker you will find this out. Kind eyes, cold eyes, mischievous eyes, indifferent eyes, eyes signalling well done, eyes letting you know that they disagree with you, and eyes closed. Eye small talk is easily read and gives you an appreciation of the reception of your message. As you deliberately and slowly move your gaze around to embrace as much of your audience as possible, you will soon appreciate the optical energy reflecting encouragement and enthusiasm.

How to use eye contact

- Use open body language and look directly at people as you make eye contact. Make sure your eyes welcome theirs.
- If it is appropriate to your speech, smile. A smile lighting the eyes lifts the spirits of the listener.
- Look for the friendly eyes in the audience.
- Many speakers recommend sweeping your eyes across the audience in either a Z, M, X or W pattern. I find that this is just one thing too many for me to manage while speaking, but this suggestion may work well for you – so consider it when you are rehearsing. I find that I naturally move my eyes around the room without using any particular pattern. Do whatever is comfortable for you.
- Do not maintain the contact too long with one particular person. This can make them feel that they are in some way

responsible for your performance and they may feel embarrassed or uncomfortable. Invariably if you look too long they will move their eyes away. Remember, it is simply making contact, but should be long enough for a basic acknowledgment of the contact before moving on to the next member of the audience.

- When you see the occasional blank or glazed eyes it may well be that those people have a million things on their minds. They are definitely not on your wavelength. Move your eyes away from them, as they will sap your energy.

I was once advised not to think about the audience while giving a speech, but to focus on a point above their heads. This is poor advice; never speak to the air above the heads of your audience. Besides making the delivery of your speech flat, it can be unsettling for your audience. You need the response from the audience to energise you. As you respond to them your presentation lifts.

Some people suggest thinking of the audience as naked or as small children. I have not had much success with either of these suggestions. I find them too distracting, as I am busy trying to mentally undress the audience or shrink them to a childlike state. It is not the audience who should be seen as naked – rather you are the one who should be baring your all to them. It is much more honest and effective to face the moment eyeball to eyeball.

Dealing with a difficult audience

The majority of audiences aren't contrary for the sake of it. There are normally many different reasons why they might appear to you, the speaker, as difficult. This might be due to the environment of the venue, misinterpreted motives of the speaker or event, poor listening skills, language difficulties or poor programming.

CELEBRITY TIP

Never begin speaking without absolute quiet in the room. Welcome the audience and *wait* till you have their undivided attention before you begin. A good trick is to either bring the lighting down in a room or take it up to full power before you begin.

Connect with your audience! Look around the room like you're talking to only one or two friends. Be as natural as possible, bringing out your personality. The more natural you are, the more relaxed you'll seem to the audience.

DEBORAH HUTTON

Preparation is always the key to avoiding conflict. However, even when you have researched your audience and tailored your speech to meet their needs, there will still be the exceptional time when your preparation does not cover you for an unresponsive, restless or hostile audience. The solution always lies in you being focused and having the mental toughness not to allow any aberrations to unbalance you. Think of the great tennis or golf players who can play with equanimity through the most difficult of situations and come out on top. It is only when they lose their composure or focus that they lose the game.

You will find that most audiences really want you to achieve but if an individual in the audience connects for a moment with something that is, for them, a personal and deep-seated issue, they will have their reservations. Or to put it another way – if you unwittingly trigger some past episode or experience, they will automatically withdraw. As in life, you must know that in reality you are not going to win over everyone who sits in the audience. We all have our own agendas and harbour some irrational dislikes.

How you handle this is the key to your success. If you experience a negative response from one or two members of the audience, accept that this is not personal and make an immediate effort to emotionally let go of the negative moment and move on to those encouraging faces.

The unresponsive audience

- The unresponsive audience is what it says – the audience gives very little back, and this has a debilitating effect on you as a speaker.
- You may never know why they are demoralised; it may well be multiple reasons – it is too hot, too soon after lunch, the program is too busy, the lighting of the venue is not good, the feng shui aspects of the location are poor, the previous speaker depleted the audience's energy, you may be the warm-up speaker for the day, the sound system does not work as well as it should, and so on. But you can be sure that the majority of these reasons have absolutely nothing to do with you and what you are about to say.
- You need to recognise that this response is not personal and emotionally switch off from this negative energy.
- To achieve in this climate, you will need to search for those friendly eyes. They may be less in number but invariably as you speak they will become more. So keep making eye contact across the audience until they start to respond. Positive eye contact supplies positive life energy to the speaker every time.

The restless audience

- A restless audience is normally the sign of a bored audience. Maybe they have been sitting too long, maybe speakers before you have gone over time. Maybe the planned agenda is too busy and they simply need a break. If you inherit such an audience then I suggest you will have a fair idea of this on the way to the platform. Consider the following hint for refreshing them:

You need to first acknowledge that it has been a long day or too hot or too exciting or there has been too much information conveyed in one sitting. Then ask them to stand and stretch for no more than thirty seconds. Ask them to resume their seats and wait patiently for them to settle before starting your speech.

- You can always use the extended pause effectively if the audience continues to show signs of restlessness.

The hostile audience

The hostile audience is very different from an unresponsive or bored audience and, fortunately, few speakers will confront this style of audience in their speaking career. You will certainly get a response from this audience. Often you can prepare for a hostile audience beforehand. If your presentation has been publicised or promoted to a wider audience, you can anticipate that there will invariably be people with differing convictions present.

Look at what you can do ahead. Try to avoid making it an 'us versus them' situation. Go through your presentation and adjust it to find some sort of common ground early in the speech that enables you to reach your audience in a logical and courteous manner.

You need to stand firm, especially if hostile questions or hecklers are interrupting you. If the meeting is being chaired, it is the responsibility of the Chair to intervene if the situation gets out of hand, but you as the speaker can use some of the following techniques to ease the pressure.

- Never lose your cool. Watch your body language; it needs to reflect a confident posture. Lose your temper and you will lose the audience's sympathy. Use the extended pause to quieten the audience.
- When someone interrupts with an aggressive comment or question, shift your eye contact away from them immediately. Continue talking and using eye contact with the rest

of the audience. If this happens at question time, use the same technique of shifting attention away from the aggressive questioner. Paraphrase their question (in less hostile words) to the audience and answer the question as truthfully as possible, while trying to tie it back into the essence of your speech. By repeating their question and trying to answer it to the best of ability you will often defuse the situation. Do not try to placate the questioner or negate your answer by saying 'I hope that answers your question'. You do not want to give them any room to continue the hostilities.

- Humour is the best tension breaker. Audiences love humour, but at your expense, definitely not theirs or the aggressor's, so if you can turn the situation with a light remark or gentle witticism use it to your advantage. Humour also makes you more accessible to the audience, and is more likely to disarm a hostile questioner.

Never lose your cool ...
Lose your temper and you will
lose the audience's sympathy.

Very, very occasionally, no matter what you do, the audience is determined that you should not be heard. In this situation the object is to retire with as much dignity intact as you can and realise that no matter what you have to say the audience are not going to give it a fair hearing. I was present at such a meeting a few years ago when our local community, buoyed by an angry lobby group, strongly protested at the possibility of having the American television series *Baywatch* filmed at a local beach. The audience were so hostile that they did not give the film company's spokesperson any opportunity to speak and address their concerns. In the end the noisy rabble completely overruled any opportunity for democracy in the decision-making process. The only thing that the council representatives and the producers could do was to leave the meeting.

Managing question time

Question time is another area with the potential for difficulties and it can become a minefield for new speakers. Below are some suggestions to help you maintain your composure as you are being questioned.

- As you prepare your presentation, review the risk areas and anticipate questions accordingly. Be a realist and expect that there will be questions or differences of opinion to your stance. Define your answers to any possible problem or clarification issues so that you have these clearly in mind.

- Make sure you listen to the question carefully and then repeat the question to the audience. Often, if there is not an additional microphone, the audience is left in the dark and only hears your answer – that will definitely make them restless.

- If the questioner is not hostile, make sure that you maintain eye contact with them during your reply.

- If the questioner is hostile, answer the question to the wider audience and do not look at your adversary.

- Keep your answers as crisp and short as you can. If more explanation is needed, suggest that the questioner have a word with you at the conclusion of the event.

- In the event that, even though you thought you had covered every possible angle in your preparation you are asked a question to which you do not know the answer, simply apologise and say: 'While I do not know the answer to this, I will do my best to find out for you. If you'd like to see me after the presentation to give me your details, I will make sure I send that information to you.'

- Remember your body language and always try to maintain a positive, confident body posture.

- Occasionally the questioner is a stirrer, who may be more interested in scoring points than actually trying to understand the communication. Never justify your views. Take control of the situation by saying: 'While I see your point of view has merit, I am committed to my line of thinking, but thank you for your comments. Next question please.'

- If the questioner is using question time to promote their own cause and wants to take all the time in the world to do so, wait for an appropriate moment when they take breath or change tactics, thank them for their views, and move on to the next question.

Whether the audience is unresponsive, restless or hostile, or question time poses a challenge, you will need to draw on your own resources of energy to boost your confidence. This is definitely a time when anchoring, the NLP tool, is invaluable (see p. 94). Use a positive memory to carry yourself over any difficult moments that may arise during your presentation. Recall that pleasant moment or experience and press your thumb and third finger together to bring it to your consciousness.

CELEBRITY TIP

Remember to *breathe*. Before you rise to speak, try to find a few moments to focus on your breathing. Long steady inhalations through the nose, and exhalations slowly through the mouth. You can do this quietly and discreetly without anyone nearby noticing.

And when you rise to speak, there really is no need to *rush*. There is plenty of time to take a long breath before you begin. And if you remember to phrase carefully, there will be plenty of opportunity to breathe steadily during your speech. Pauses during a presentation can help its impact, so don't be afraid to pause, look around the room, make eye contact with one or two people, then return to your notes and continue.

IAN ROSS

Creating a connection with your audience is the key to successful communication no matter whether they are a responsive or difficult audience. Do this by looking directly at your audience and being aware of the underlying communication that is taking place between you. As you look you will find eyes alight with interest or encouragement and you will also find eyes that show no warmth, are glazed or focused on something other than what you have to say. Move on quickly if you encounter the disinterested and look for the bright eyes as these people will re-energise you. Make eye contact with members of the audience by slowly moving your eyes around the assembly. Look for the positive response in their eyes and then move on; do not linger as this may compromise the momentary but lively connection you have with them.

STEP 8

VOICE
MATTERS

His voice was as intimate as the rustle of sheets.

DOROTHY PARKER, *American writer and poet, 1893–1967*

Learn how to breathe properly for better voice production and try out some exercises to improve your articulation. Watch out for the rising inflection. Find out how to take care of your voice, especially if you have laryngitis.

The voice and its workings are complex physiological matters. The information presented in this chapter is general in nature and if you have any concerns about your voice you should refer to either your doctor or a speech therapist.

The voice is a wind instrument which when used effectively can create a magnificent singing or speaking voice. The quality of your voice relies on correct breathing and the ability to form rounded vowels and clear consonants with the tongue, mouth and jaw. Your voice also needs to have energy. This energy is fuelled by that all-important element of enthusiasm.

The sound of your voice

A recent survey carried out by the Center for Voice Disorders at Wake Forest University in North Carolina to find the Best and Worst Voices in America identified Earle Nightingale, Sean Connery, Julia Roberts, Barbra Streisand, Mel Gibson, Meg Ryan and Anthony Hopkins among the top ten Best Voices. The Worst Voices list included Fran Drescher, Roseanne Barr, Joan Rivers, Mike Tyson and Rosie O'Donnell, as well as several radio show hosts. The survey results showed that Americans prefer melodious, low-pitched voices. They did not like voices that were high-pitched (obviously this was relative to gender), especially if the voice had a screechy quality.

For some people the voice is instrumental in their passage to financial and personal success – consider, for example, the mellow tones of radio broadcasters John Laws, Margaret Throsby, Merrick and Rosso, or the anonymous voice-over tones in advertising that entreat us to buy, watch or listen to products and events. These voices resonate with the desired low-pitched smoothness.

Think back to trademark voices that we instantly recognise. Through years of exposure to them on our screens we have grown to appreciate every utterance and expression of these branded voices. Remember the Marlborough smoke-etched voice of John Wayne, the crisp Anglo-American modulation of Cary Grant, the explosive punctuation of James Cagney, the stretched articulation of Katharine Hepburn, the breathy little-girl voice of Marilyn Monroe and the so-slow but so-smooth drawl of James Stewart.

Not everyone gets a James Stewart or Katharine Hepburn voice card handed to them at birth. However, with a bit of effort, the voice you have can be improved whether it is simply through the power of its projection or the production qualities of resonance and pitch. There is no doubt that the voice affects how people perceive you as a speaker. You can look a billion dollars but when you open your mouth to speak if the voice is high-pitched, raspy or articulately lazy you can undo the Armani image in seconds.

A word here on stammering: in my experience and reading, it is clear that many stammerers are high achievers and often put themselves into the situation of public speaking. I have a friend who is good public speaker. She has overcome many obstacles in order to stand up in front of an audience and, I can assure you, she does not get the sympathy vote; she makes it on her own merits.

There have been great speakers who have suffered a speech impediment or stutter – Sir Winston Churchill, King George Vl and Dr Jonathan Miller from the ABC series *The Body in Question*. Stutterers will tell you that they have to be at least twenty words ahead of themselves to replace the stumbling block word with a different word or phrase that they know they can handle. Perhaps this is why they are so bright, as their minds are always looking for solutions. So if you have a stammer you are in good company. Don't let it stop you from achieving a goal of public speaking if this is what you want to do. A good way to hone your speaking potential is to join a supportive speaking club such as Toastmasters or an International Training in Communication Club.

Most people who hear their voice on tape for the first time are, at worst shocked, and at best amazed, at how different their voice sounds from what they have imagined. I think it is fairly normal that most of us do not like our voice the first time we hear it on a recording. But generally you will find this comes from the fact that we are used to hearing a different sound when we speak.

The speaking voice emanates from the larynx which is driven by the breath before being modified in the mouth, nose and throat where the tongue, palate, cheek and lips articulate the sound. The larynx is a pretty busy junction attached to the trachea. Its functions include breathing, swallowing and speaking, as well as less exciting functions such as vomiting. A man's larynx is about 20 per cent larger than a woman's, which is why their Adam's apple is more pronounced.

If you are in a career that demands you take centre stage consistently – for example, you are an actor, barrister, trainer, tour guide, teacher or professional speaker – it may serve you well to undertake some voice training. Before doing this, I recommend that you visit a speech therapist to make sure that you are not abusing your vocal cords in any way; then look at taking some singing lessons with a view to improving your speaking voice. Contact your local chapter of the Australian National Association of Teachers of Singing to find a teacher suitable for your needs and within your vicinity. The teacher must be willing to coach you for speaking purposes rather than focusing on singing.

Can you change your voice? Clearly, the equipment we get at birth is what we have to work with. For the vast majority of us this will suffice and with proper care will do us great service over our lifetime. But if you want to change or enrich your voice you can, although it does take consistent practice. A proper breathing technique can improve your lung capacity by up to 60 per cent, which in turn will improve your voice production and voice projection. Good breathing technique requires you to breathe from the diaphragm, rather than from the chest. When we are born we breathe naturally from the diaphragm, which is why a baby's cry is so loud.

The following sections on how to breathe using the diaphragm and the benefits of breathing this way and using breath management to control performance anxiety have been contributed by my friend and colleague, Marlene Vaughan.

Marlene is a singer and stage performer, as well as a drama and public-speaking teacher.

Improve your voice production with diaphragmatic breathing

Most of the time our breathing is automatic and as such it is a fairly unthinking procedure. This passive breathing allows only about one-tenth of the total amount of air in the lungs to pass in and out. In speech, the force of the breath passing the vocal cords produces the vocal sound. To avoid straining the voice, the amount and strength with which the breath passes the vocal cords should be directed from the lower lobes of the lungs. Some people refer to this as diaphragmatic breathing.

The diaphragm is an involuntary muscle which responds to the amount of breath that is present in the lungs. When you breathe out, the diaphragm rises up in the chest cavity and as you breathe in, due to the expansion of the lungs, the diaphragm moves down and flattens out under the lungs.

The diaphragm can be toned by exercise. Climbing mountains will tone the diaphragm in response to the deeper breathing that is necessary in such physical exercise. Or you can do breathing exercises to improve the breath support system.

In public speaking, voice production is a total body experience, starting with good posture, which is paramount to a well-modulated speaking voice. Once good posture is achieved, deep diaphragmatic breathing can be achieved. Remember that both flexibility and its opposite, rigidity, can be detected in the vocal tone.

The shortcomings of shallow breathing

Shallow, nose or throat breathing, also known as clavicular breathing, uses only a small portion of the lung capacity and is usually evidenced by a raising of the shoulders on the inhalation.

Often the effect of this shallow breathing is that it causes the speaker to have a very high-pitched, sometimes nasal tone, which is not very attractive. The speaker can become breathless and unable to complete lengthy passages without struggling for breath or even gasping in mid-phrase. The speaker will also lack verbal dexterity due to shortness of breath and be unable to control pitch, tone and resonance.

The benefits of capacity breathing

In complete breath/capacity/diaphragmatic breathing the chest cavity is increased to its normal limits in all directions and every part of the machinery functions and performs its natural work. As a result, the speaker experiences increased vocal dexterity, tone and pitch. They will not need to gasp for breath and will be able to complete lengthy phrases. Consequently they will be a more credible speaker with a well-modulated, resonant voice that will be a pleasure to listen to.

It is not necessary to breathe to the full capacity of the lungs all the time. But to achieve any improvement in the voice, the full complete breath should be practised daily as follows.

How to carry out capacity breathing

- Stand with your feet comfortably apart, relax the shoulders and lift the sternum (chest bone), ensure that your chin is not jutting out or tucked too far in, forcing the head out of alignment with the spine.
- Breathe in through the nostrils without raising your shoulders, and feel the breath as it expands the lower lobes of the lungs. Notice that as you continue to inhale the abdomen will expand, as will the ribs, allowing the air to fill the mid-lobes of the lungs and as you complete the inhalation there is a sensation of air filling the upper lungs.

- In exhaling notice how the abdomen, then ribs, and finally the chest, slowly fall as the breath is expelled. The complete breath is akin to pouring water into and out of a bottle. The water fills the lower section of the bottle first and then the mid-section and finally the upper section. Likewise, when you up-end the bottle to pour the water out, the lower part of the bottle is emptied first, then the mid-section and finally the water in the upper section of the bottle pours out.

- Now place your hands around the lower ribs with your thumbs pointing towards the spine and repeat the capacity breathing exercise. This time as you exhale try to hold the ribs out and repeat inhalations and exhalations while maintaining this posture by using the muscles between the ribs (the intercostal muscles). Don't use force, just a gentle control. Relax completely after three or four repetitions so that you do not overtax these muscles.

- When you feel comfortable with this process add sounds such as 'Haaaa' or 'Sssss' as you exhale. Increase the repetitions daily till it becomes very easy to maintain the position for extended periods and replace the sounds with passages of dialogue.

Avoid overbreathing at all costs; there should be no force either on the inhalation or the exhalation. It is best not to think about controlling the breath or the muscles; only lift the sternum and 'open' the body to the inspiration. Management rather than control is the key. The muscles of the abdomen are not to be pulled in or pushed out but should be allowed to respond naturally to the process of inhalation and exhalation.

This method of breathing has also been termed 'appoggio' by the Italianate school. 'Appoggio' can be translated as 'support' as the actual Italian verb means 'to lean upon'. The technique itself is best explained by the act of leaning upon the ribs in order to maintain their expanded position. To master this technique one must use gentle pressure via the intercostal muscles and the sensation should be of expansion without tension.

Breath management and performance anxiety

As mentioned in Step 6, Managing Stage Fright (pp. 87–97), it is well known that an increased rate of breathing is associated with anxiety. In high-anxiety situations some people can hyperventilate. The antidote for this is to breathe into a paper bag in an attempt to re-ingest carbon dioxide and find a balance between the levels of oxygen and carbon dioxide to help slow down the breathing. As breathing is brought under control the emotions too can be better managed. By consciously slowing down the rate of breathing you can lessen anxiety (see Calming Deep Breathing, p. 95). This is handy for public speaking, as performance anxiety can become a problem.

A certain amount of heightened emotion is expected in performance situations. This can be either energy-enhancing or energy-sapping. If one employs proper breath management techniques the energy can be well managed and directed and becomes a positive tool in communication.

The capacity or diaphragmatic breath has also been called by yogis the 'bellows breath' as not only does it mirror the movement of air in the bellows, but it can also fan the fires of the solar plexus, which in yogi circles is known as the seat of energy in the body. Energy is an important component of performance and gives that added edge in public speaking, which facilitates communication between the speaker and his or her audience.

Improve your articulation

When I was growing up in London, it was the done thing to speak 'BBC English' which was the loosely described 'plum in the mouth' pronunciation used by BBC announcers at that time. Regional dialects were frowned upon and I remember my mother constantly correcting the slightest hint of 'East Ender' overtones in my speech. Today, thank goodness, we are free of such thinking and can appreciate different accents without judging the speaker.

Articulation, the capacity to speak clearly and distinctly, is the key. No matter what the accent or how attractive it is, if you are not crisping those consonants or forming those vowels, your speech will lack power and possibly be misheard.

It is easy to become complacent about how clearly we speak, especially in today's busy world. I have always thought that I pronounced my name, 'Mary Atkins', clearly enough for people to understand but just recently when I have said my name on the phone, several people have thought that I have said 'Mary Anne'!

So listen to yourself on a tape recording and, once you have overcome your initial reaction, play the tape again to make sure you are pronouncing words clearly. It is important to listen carefully to make sure you are not mumbling or slurring your words. If you do not have a tape recorder, ask a friend to critique you honestly. Vowels and consonants should be identifiable, unlike the speaking voice of the late Dean Martin, the actor, singer and straight-guy partner to Jerry Lewis, who rarely sounded a consonant and rolled most of his words over into the next word.

Tongue twisters to tease and please

Tongue twisters are marvellously wicked little phrases and rhymes that make your whole mouth work. They are invaluable if you have trouble getting your tongue around certain sounds. I have trouble with the words 'thief' and 'froth', so I am happy to have some fun with tongue twisters that loosen my lips, tongue and jaws.

Start slowly at first, as you say the twister over and over, gathering speed as you progress. If you are driving to your speaking assignment, choose your favourites to practise on the way.

Red leather, yellow leather
Red lorry, yellow lorry
Good blood, bad blood
Buttah, guttah, guttah, buttah
Sixish, sixish, sixish
Six sick slick slim sycamore saplings
Two toads terribly tired trying to trot to Tilbury
Crisp crusts crackle crunchily
Fat frogs flying past fast
A dozen double damask dinner napkins
Knapsack straps
Lovely lemon liniment
Nine night nurses nursing nicely
Many an anemone sees an enemy anemone
Six thick thistle sticks. Six thick thistles stick.
Friday's five fresh fish specials
Around the rugged rocks the ragged rascal ran

How much wood would a woodchuck chuck
If a woodchuck could chuck wood?
He would chuck, he would, as much as he could,
And chuck as much wood as a woodchuck would
If a woodchuck could chuck wood.

I'm not the pheasant plucker,
I'm the pheasant plucker's mate.
I'm only plucking pheasants
'Cause the pheasant plucker's late.

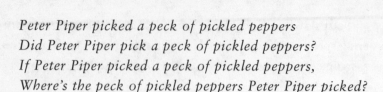

Peter Piper picked a peck of pickled peppers
Did Peter Piper pick a peck of pickled peppers?
If Peter Piper picked a peck of pickled peppers,
Where's the peck of pickled peppers Peter Piper picked?

Other warm-up exercises

If you can find a quiet place to practise these before you speak then do, but if not, do the 'noise' elements on your way to the venue.

- Relax your mouth, neck and shoulders. Shrug your shoulders a few times and stretch your neck right up and then relax it.
- Make a prolonged 'prrrrr' sound through relaxed lips.
- Spread the lips in a smile and say 'eeeee' and close them to say 'ooooo'. Repeat several times.
- Grin and pout, grin and pout. Repeat several times – do it with attitude and you have a good Mick Jagger impersonation!
- Do a huge yawn. (This exercise is one you can definitely do before your speech but make sure you do not yawn when another speaker is strutting their stuff.)
- Massage your chin and the big muscles either side of your neck. (Massaging your chin is an ideal way to counteract a dry mouth as it stimulates saliva flow.)

The rising inflection

We touched on this in the previous chapter but as it is such a common feature of Australian speech, will look at it again here. When a speaker lifts their words or tone at the end of a sentence, the statement becomes a question. As the speaker changes rhythm and pitch to facilitate this, the tenor of the speech takes on a sing-song characteristic. The audience focus their attention and anticipation on the next rise and fall of words and phrases and do not appreciate the quality of the message. The speaker loses credibility and their words lose impact.

Throughout the English-speaking world it seems that the rising inflection is gaining prominence – it largely seems to be a female tendency. Perhaps it reflects women's lack of confidence in their opinions. Unfortunately, the rising inflection is very much a national signature style of speech for many Australians. We do it without thinking in our everyday conversations – face-to-face, on the telephone, in that all-important interview. We simply do not hear it. We are not aware we are doing it.

When we stand on a podium we need to be free of it. So it is back to the recorded tape of your voice or that honest friend to listen carefully for any hint of that upward tone.

How to rid yourself of a rising inflection

- Identify that you speak with a rising inflection.
- Say a sentence still using the rising inflection – hear it, be aware of how you feel when you are doing it.
- Now practise the same sentence, concentrating on keeping the pitch of those last few words down.
- Keep practising the downward fall at the end of the sentence until you are very aware of the difference in your style of speech.
- Record yourself if you can, so you can hear the difference in your voice in a rising inflection and in a lowering inflection.
- It takes time to break a habit, so keep being aware of your speech and keep practising to pull those last words in the statement downwards.

Taking care of your voice

- Keep the larynx hydrated. Drink lots of water, at least eight glasses a day. The water should be at room temperature, never chilled.

- Don't smoke.
- Sleep is a vital element in maintaining the overall good health of the voice.
- Avoid talking over loud noises.
- Avoid dairy products on the day of the speech as they may create mucus.
- Avoid caffeine or any other kind of drugs (unless prescribed) before you perform.
- If you can, eat at least an hour before you speak. If you are the 'after-dinner' speaker then eat very lightly and give yourself time to go to the bathroom to do some discreet warm-up exercises.
- Avoid, where you can, excessive throat clearing and coughing.
- If you are speaking at an air-conditioned venue, be aware that the air-conditioning will dry out the larynx and make sure you keep drinking plenty of water – room temperature, not chilled.
- If you have a heavy speaking day, rest the larynx whenever you can. Sit and read a book.
- If you are speaking outside to a group, make sure you get them close together so that you do not have to strain to make yourself heard and never walk and talk while trying to manage a group.

If you are suffering from laryngitis or hoarseness

- The best way to recover from laryngitis is to stop using your voice so that the swelling can subside. Stay completely quiet.
- Don't whisper or clear your throat if you have laryngitis – it will just make it worse. Whispering puts more stress on the vocal cords.
- Instead of whispering, speak in a normal voice at a lower volume and do not try to compete with background noises, such as other people talking.

- Avoid coughing and drink a lot of water to keep the body hydrated. If hoarseness is related to a cold, don't use cold medications, which can dry the throat.

- Drink at least eight to ten glasses of water a day. This ensures that your larynx stays moist, a key step in curing laryngitis. The water should be warm or room temperature. Don't add salt or alcohol. You can substitute juice or warm tea with honey for water.

- Drink even more if you're flying, because the air you breathe in planes is very drying.

- People with voice problems that persist for more than two weeks should visit their doctor.

CELEBRITY TIP

I always take hot water, lemon and honey, as it coats the throat and the lemon cuts any mucus that gets in the way of my voice being clear.

TONI CHILDS

While you cannot change the basic sound of your voice, you can train your voice to improve its volume and flexibility. Using the diaphragmatic breathing method will enrich your speaking and the command of your performance. Your vocal cords function better when fully hydrated, so drink plenty of water, preferably at room temperature, as this temperature is kinder to your larynx. To articulate well you need to 'warm up' the mouth and jaw by doing some simple mouth and jaw exercises before speaking. Tongue twisters also help to loosen the tongue and lips. Remember to avoid the 'rising inflection' at all costs. Taking care of your voice at all times is essential but when you have a little hoarseness or laryngitis, the best way is to 'zip the lip' and avoid speaking until you are better.

USING AUDIOVISUAL EQUIPMENT

Some microphones work great as long as you blow into them. So you stand there like an idiot blowing and saying 'Are we on? Can you hear me?' Everyone admits that they can hear you blowing. It's only when you speak that the microphone goes dead.

ERMA BOMBECK, *If Life is a Bowl of Cherries – What am I doing in the Pits?*

Understand the basics of using a variety of microphones, an overhead projector, writing on a whiteboard or butcher's paper, using a teleprompter and delivering a dynamic PowerPoint presentation.

This chapter is designed to give you an easy reference on how to use a variety of audiovisual (AV) equipment. Unless you are an audiovisual technician, there is nothing sexy about AV tools but when you are communicating to a crowd they are a necessary part of speech-making that must be understood and used effectively.

> **CELEBRITY TIP**
>
> Always do a sound, lighting and equipment check beforehand. Meet the people responsible and work with them to make it perfect. These three things, if not done correctly, have the power to kill a great presentation.
>
> Make sure the audience can see you properly and you can read your notes. Be sure the sound level is clear and high enough to sustain a room *full* of people.
>
> Double-check any visual aids – breakdowns often occur and you'll be the one looking unprofessional.
>
> DEBORAH HUTTON

Starting with the all-important sound system, you will find there are several types of microphones that you may encounter. Other important skills you may need to master could include writing boldly on a whiteboard or on butcher's paper, putting the transparencies the right way up on an overhead projector, learning how to produce a jazzy PowerPoint presentation smoothly on the big screen or delivering a presentation using a teleprompter.

The sophistication and quality of the equipment you use will vary. If you are speaking at a conference you could well enjoy state-of-the-art facilities, complete with a sound technician. If you speak at your local service club you may be lucky to have a microphone, lectern and possibly be able to use an overhead projector and whiteboard. At some venues you might only get a portable sound box. You will need to be flexible in your approach to voice amplification and visual aids.

Check and double-check equipment

The first rule when dealing with audiovisual paraphernalia is to give yourself plenty of time before the event starts to check and try out the equipment. The last thing you want to deal with as you stand up to speak is equipment that doesn't work. Even when there is a promise of a sound technician on hand, don't be complacent. As a conference organiser I have seen the most accomplished and experienced speaker arrive without their PowerPoint presentation on a disk. One speaker who knew they would be running a little late on the day even sent the wrong disk in the mail to the technician before the conference – the technician loaded this in good faith. I am sure I don't need to spell out the consequences.

So, no matter what the circumstances, arrive early, check and double-check. If you are speaking at an event or conference where you are working with a professional conference organiser (PCO), the earlier you can get material to them the less risk you run of making mistakes. Generally the PCO will check this against your speaker's paper (provided you have submitted one) and once the audiovisual technicians have downloaded your material you can check with them that the material is right and works efficiently.

I recently went as a guest to the most fantastic event (or so I was told)! My reservations were not in any way to do with the quality of speakers, whom I believe were excellent, but rather with the quality of the sound or rather the lack of it. The sound system worked well in the front half of the room but was non-existent at the back of the room. During the two hours of speeches, the audience indicated frequently that they could not hear the speakers. Instead of stopping procedures to get the hotel management team to correct it, the organisers continued, presumably in the hope that either the sound system would eventually work or if they got the speaker to shout loudly enough into the microphones they could be heard.

The poor management of the sound system undermined the credibility of this organisation. This problem no doubt could have easily been fixed if the speakers had tested the micro-phones beforehand and asked their colleagues to place themselves around the room while they tested the sound levels.

Knowing only too well how much perspiration, inspiration, courage and time is involved in getting yourself to the podium, I agonise when a speaker is prepared to have all this fail, simply because of the lack of that extra 5 per cent of effort that it takes to check and test the equipment.

The second rule with audiovisual equipment is that there are no grey areas: it either works or it doesn't (or it is either there or it isn't). Leave nothing to chance – check, recheck and test equipment; never, ever trust untested audiovisual equipment.

Rule number three is to always have an alternative game plan in case the equipment fails. I recommend you take as a back-up a secondary PowerPoint disk of your presentation and for double security, your presentation transposed onto overhead transparencies.

Microphone techniques

There are many different types of microphones. Emile Berliner who worked with Alexander Graham Bell invented the microphone in 1827. The carbon microphone is the oldest and simplest and is still used in some telephones today. Other types of microphones that have been invented since then include the electromagnet dynamic microphone, ribbon microphone, con-denser microphone and crystal microphone. Which is all riveting stuff and very useful if you ever need microphone info at a Trivia night but for speaking that is information overload. We just need to know how to use it.

There are many people and speakers who are microphone-phobic. They recoil in horror at the mention of using a micro-phone. They prefer instead to strain their voice in an effort to be heard. The microphone does not have any sinister influences (except when it doesn't work); it merely amplifies the sound comfortably throughout the length and breadth of the venue. You simply speak into it, in your normal speaking voice, as though you were speaking one to one and it will do the rest.

If you can push past the phobia always say 'yes please' to the use of a microphone as it puts less strain on you and the audience. Remember, the audience should be paramount in your communications – if they cannot hear your words clearly you might as well pack up shop, because your words will 'fall on deaf ears'.

Using different microphones

MICROPHONE ON A STAND (EITHER LEAD OR RADIO TYPE)

- You should know how to change the height of the microphone. Most stands are adjustable by a simple screw mechanism that allows you to lengthen or shorten the height of the stand before tightening the flange, which will hold it in the right position.
- Always make sure that the microphone is at the right height for you. It should be at mid-chin height. The microphone should directly face you and you should position yourself about a hand-span away from it.
- Normally the on/off switch is situated on the side of the microphone itself.
- Sometimes you can remove the microphone so it becomes a hand-held microphone. If it can be removed you will just need to clip it off. If you want to move around the stage and the microphone has a lead, make sure there is sufficient lead to do this, keeping the lead firmly behind so that you do not trip over it as you move.

BUILT-IN LECTERN MICROPHONE

- Normally built-in microphones cannot be removed from the lectern. They have a sprung gooseneck that can be bent to the height you need.
- When you arrive at the lectern to speak make sure you adjust the microphone before speaking.
- The microphone should be directly facing you. Position yourself about a hand-span away, with the microphone level situated about mid-chin height.
- These microphones are normally turned on or off by the venue audio technician.
- Generally lectern microphones are found in hotels or function venues. Most of the time they work very well as they are in constant use and well maintained. Very occasionally they can be a little tricky. If, when you test them, you find any problems make sure you call in the venue management team, as they will be able to fix it or provide another microphone.

HAND-HELD MICROPHONE WITH LEAD

- This is a microphone on a lead, or as you saw in the section on stand microphones (p. 128), it could be a microphone that is simply detached from the stand.
- Make sure that the lead is long enough for you to move around and that you keep the lead behind you so that you do not trip over it as you move.
- The microphone should be held about a hand-span from your body and just below your chin. The reason this is lower is because there is a tendency for people using this type of microphone to bring it comfortably closer and closer to their mouth. When it is too close to the mouth it amplifies all the breathy 'p' and 'b' sounds to distraction.

- The on/off switch is normally situated on the side of microphone itself.

For the new speaker I suggest, where possible, that you ask for a built-in lectern microphone as this enables you to manage your notes more easily.

RADIO MICROPHONE

- The benefit of a radio mike is that there is no lead. The only time a radio microphone causes a problem is when you are speaking at a trade show or exhibition where there could be several radio microphones used in fairly close proximity. If the technician who programmed your microphone accidentally puts you on the same radio frequency as someone else, you could feasibly pick up Fred on the other side of the pavilion. Fred is selling the best potato peeler in the world and you are trying, with the addition of Fred's peeling spiel, to promote the benefits of a time-share resort plan! Solution – call the sound technician back in immediately to reprogram the frequency. Just a note here: always keep the audio technician's telephone number handy.
- As with the hand-held microphone with a lead, a radio microphone should be held about a hand-span from your body and just below your chin. Avoid bringing it too close to your mouth so that your listeners aren't bombarded with the p's and b's.
- Normally the on/off switch is situated on the microphone itself, often with a radio switch at the base of the mike. There is usually a small light on the base of the microphone next to the on/off switch that will glow 'green' when the microphone is on.
- Radio microphones run on battery power, so it is essential that the internal battery be replaced with a new one every time it is used.

HEADSET MICROPHONE

- With a headset microphone, the headset sits nicely over the head rather like an Alice band and the short bendable microphone sits to one side of the mouth. Again, this can be a radio or lead microphone. Known affectionately as the 'Madonna mike', it is invaluable for the speaker who needs to keep their hands free for a craft, cooking or other training or education demonstration or workshop.
- The headset should go over the head comfortably and position the microphone below the lips about mid-chin so it does not pick up the explosive prrrrr and brrrrr sounds.
- The on/off switch is housed in a separate control box that you can clip on over the waistband of your trousers or skirt.
- Radio microphones run on battery power, so it is essential that the internal battery be replaced with a new one every time it is used.
- Be careful with this microphone, as it is very, very tempting to pull it too close to the mouth so you pick up the staccato sounds of the consonants.
- If you are working with a lead, make sure it is always behind you. If you move be aware that it should be kept behind you.

LAPEL MICROPHONE

- The lapel microphone is my absolute favourite if you are working with a sound crew on television or a good AV team who really know their business. They wire you up for sound and test for sound levels beforehand. These are the very best of equipment and pick up the slightest sound.
- But not all microphones are equal, so if you do have to work with a lapel microphone without the benefit of a sound engineer, make sure you place it high and firmly enough on your clothing so that you are heard. Test very thoroughly and extensively beforehand.

- Like the headset microphone, a lapel microphone can be switched on or off from the separate control box that clips onto the waistband of your trousers or skirt.
- Try not to speak directly into the microphone.
- Remember, good lapel microphones will pick up sounds very easily, so take care with jewellery or hand movements.
- Be careful not to turn your head away from the side where the lapel microphone is located (that is, if the microphone is located on the left lapel, when you turn your head to the right your voice will not be heard).
- If you have doubts about the quality of the lapel microphone to be used and you are given the option of using a different microphone, always opt for either a headset microphone (if you need to move around) or a freestanding microphone whether it is on a stand or part of the lectern.

Testing a microphone

- If you are working without a sound technician make yourself fully aware of how to turn the microphone on and off. Normally the compere or emcee will have the microphone turned on and so the microphone will be live when you step up to speak. The reason I suggest you investigate this is purely as a safeguard for you. It might be that you are the first speaker. If you know how to work the microphone then it is just one less thing to worry about. If you are working with a sound technician you will not have to worry as the technician will take care of it from a central sound panel.
- While sound technicians may gently tap the microphone to test for the required response, I recommend that speakers do not tap or blow on the microphone as they are pretty delicate and expensive instruments. Simply say a few words to test its capabilities, always making sure you have someone listening to the sound levels in all parts of the room.

- In an empty space the sound will be louder than in a room full of people, so take that into account.
- If there are no professional sound people present to steer you, make sure that the sound speakers are situated well away from the microphone so that you do not experience feedback.
- The sound speakers should always be in front of the microphone to avoid feedback.
- If you are moving around on the stage make sure you do not move in front of the speakers otherwise you will experience that really horrid feedback screech.
- If it is a microphone on a stand make sure you are aware of how the stand can be adjusted.
- Practise your stance with the microphone – remember it should always be about a hand-span away from you and no higher than mid-chin level or slightly lower. Practise a few p's and b's to satisfy yourself that the microphone is not picking up these noises excessively. If it is, adjust the microphone again.

What to do if the microphone fails

- If the microphone fails during your performance, get the organiser to find someone to fix it or get a substitute mike. If it is a small venue and crowd, move off the stage to get closer to the body of the audience so that you can simply project your voice until you are rescued. Whenever things go wrong, make light of it to the audience, before continuing with your speech.
- If the venue or hall is very large and you are speaking to a large audience, do not attempt to work without a mike. Move off the stage and wait until it is fixed. If the wait is long, decide on a strategy with the organiser for the progression or restart of your presentation.

Using an overhead projector

The overhead projector must have been every teacher and lecturer's favourite before the age of the PC and PowerPoint presentations. For some speakers and lecturers, it is still their preferred way of presenting information. Once you have mastered the on/off switch, it is a reasonably foolproof way of presenting. It has the added advantage that the presenter can add to their printed material or present the results of conclusions to the audience by using a water-based overhead pen to write on the acetate sheet or transparency. Acetate sheets are easily accessible; most newsagents carry them and they are inexpensive to buy.

I recommend that you carry a set of transparencies with you as a back-up to a PowerPoint presentation. The odd occasion does arise when even though you have checked the compatibility of equipment that will be available to you a glitch can occur with either your or the AV team's software or hardware. If you have your presentation on transparencies you can deliver it just as effectively. Like taking an umbrella with you on a fine day, it almost guarantees that it will not rain.

Tips for preparing a transparency

- Use a font like Arial or Helvetica as these letters are clean and easy to read.
- Use a large font – maximum 40-point size for the title and a minimum 26-point for bullet-point information.
- Use a minimum amount of information on each sheet – no more than seven lines on a page and no more than seven words on a line. These should be key points that you wish to make. Edit and re-edit so that you achieve strong, memorable statements.

- Print off copies of each slide on paper. Use these as you present. You can add any additional notes to these copies which will act as memory prompts.
- You can photocopy black and white or colour graphics, pictures or cartoons to illustrate a point. Remember, if you are using material that is not yours, always check that you may use the material and of course you must acknowledge the author or creator.
- Always carry some spare transparencies and water-based marker pens.
- Place the transparency in a clear sleeve with fold-out flaps, which act as a frame when using it on the projector.

Presenting effectively, using the overhead projector

- Use the on/off switch to control the presentation. Switch off to place the transparency on and then switch on, switch off to remove, and so on. Overhead projectors are designed to be switched off and on repeatedly, so get into the habit of turning the machine off between transparencies. Leave them on and you are simply lighting the room and running the risk of overheating the projector and blowing the lamp. Leaving it on between transparencies can be distracting as when you move the slide you have a wall or screen of very bright white light.
- Turning the projector off is great for bringing the audience's attention back to you.
- Use the transparency on the projector or your notes on the copy as your memory prompter. Never turn your back to the audience to read from the screen.
- If you want the audience to receive the information in small increments, use a sheet of paper, an envelope or a card to mask the information. Slide it down to expose the material line by line.

- If you are right-handed, stand to the left of the projector to present and change transparencies or stand to the right if you are left-handed.
- If you need to point at something on the transparency use a narrow pen rather than your finger. Lay the pointer on the transparency to get a good crisp image.
- If you have a very long and involved presentation you might want to ask the organiser to change your slides for you while you present from the lectern. Make sure that you give them a copy of the presentation and that this is in perfect order. Remember to cue them in where and when you want the next slide. Make sure that the cue is discreet and does not detract from your message. Presenters often forget about the person changing their slides and get off track so that the slides do not match with what they are saying. Remember to cue the next slide at the right time.
- Always check the equipment beforehand. Request that a spare lamp be available just in case and where possible a back-up overhead projector.

What to do if the overhead projector fails

If all your forward planning fails and you have a faulty projector that cannot be fixed, then you will have to present from the lectern. Remember to make a joke of it to the audience and refuse to let it throw you off-balance. Life is like that – just when you thought you had it all together, the light goes out! Obviously you will have to think on your feet, as you will not have any visual aids to progress the speech. Being prepared is the best insurance, so as you prepare your presentation get a mental word picture of how to describe the graphic or visual.

PowerPoint presentations

The majority of speakers at conferences tend to rely on a PowerPoint presentation. Of all the visual aids this is the most flexible and least obtrusive. You can take centre stage with your laptop sited just off-centre and a wireless remote control in your hand. Your audience will not know that your laptop supplies the crib sheet information that dramatically splashes on the screen.

With a PowerPoint presentation you can use background colour to influence the emotion or the theme of the presentation. You can make it sexier with film, music or relevant charts and graphics.

Computer hardware and software capabilities are changing almost day by day. You can purchase software specific for PowerPoint to make designing your presentation easier and more dynamic. If you are looking for more specific information there are quite a few computer magazines available at newsagents, a good place to start your investigation. As computer software changes so rapidly, I will provide only basic hints and tips for making the most of presenting with PowerPoint here.

Tips for preparing a PowerPoint presentation

- Use a font like Ariel or Helvetica as these letters are clean and easy to read.
- Use a large font – maximum 40-point size for the title and a minimum 26-point for bullet-point information.
- Use a minimum amount of information on each sheet – no more than seven lines on a page and no more than seven words on a line. These should be key points that you wish to make. Edit and re-edit to achieve strong, memorable statements.
- Avoid using all capital letters as they are more difficult to read.
- Keep the background simple; use a coloured background to subtly influence your audience. A dark background (for example, deep blue) with light-coloured text (for example, white) works effectively.
- Use colour to highlight and convey mood and feeling. Blue says trust me, truth and justice. Green denotes growth.

Yellow indicates confidence, warmth and wisdom. Grey says integrity and maturity. Red excites and alerts. (But don't use red text; it is too hard to read.)

- Insert photographs, flow charts, graphics, music, maps, tables or plans to add to the texture and interest of your presentation. Remember the old saying that a picture is worth a thousand words and use it to your advantage when you are compiling your material.

Tips for delivering a PowerPoint presentation

- Stand at the side of the screen and place your laptop so that you can read each slide easily.
- Use a wire-less or lead remote control to control your slide show.
- Never turn your back to the audience.
- Never read the slide – flesh out the key statements to make it come to life.
- Use a laser pointer to highlight information.
- Make sure you check the compatibility of equipment available or bring your own laptop.
- As a back-up, always carry your presentation on disk.
- Print out transparencies where possible as a back-up and always print a hard copy in case you need to use it. If the worst happens, you will be able to present from the lectern using your notes.
- Rehearse your presentation frequently until you find you can anticipate each slide and are ready with the spiel.
- You can give your presentation on CD to the venue AV technician to 'drive' for you. If so, ask the venue for a 'chairman's buzzer'. This is a small button linked to the venue technician's desk which when pressed will trigger a cue light, informing the technician to advance to the next slide.

Working with a teleprompter

A teleprompter or autocue is a device that is most commonly used in television studios for newsreaders or show hosts but has moved into the domain of major business presentations and other large events where the accuracy of material presented is paramount to the overall success of the function.

A teleprompter allows the speaker to see a reflected script of their speech, which is generated from a computer terminal located offstage. The teleprompter operator scrolls the script at the speaking pace of the speaker. If the equipment is sophisticated the script appears on several glass reflectors that are located just below the speaker's eye level so that it looks as if the speaker is looking directly at the audience as they move their head around. A less sophisticated version provides a screen monitor, which is placed below eye level. This obviously does not allow the flexibility of the more expensive version.

Teleprompters allow you to see about four or five lines of copy at a time and the operator carefully follows the script to make sure that the script keeps at the presenter's pace at all times.

If you are considering using the teleprompter at an event you need to:

- Prepare a typewritten script. Check with the teleprompter operator to find out if there are any specific instructions for font or format and whether they prefer to save it to disk.
- Give the typescript to the teleprompter operator in plenty of time.
- Ensure that you have at least one rehearsal as a minimum guide, two would be preferable, with the operator so that they can appreciate your pace and so that you get used to the scrolling.
- Make sure that you are comfortable using the glass reflectors or screen.

- Don't fixate on the reflectors or screen while you are presenting. Move your head as though you are making eye contact with the audience.
- Always carry your script with you to the lectern as a safeguard in case the equipment fails.

Using a whiteboard, chalkboard or butcher's paper

Generally whiteboards or butcher's paper are used in a workshop setting. They allow you to record information and use this information strategically. The degree of sophistication of whiteboards will vary from a freestanding, simple whiteboard and easel to a Rolls Royce job that is large, mobile and has a motorised whiteboard face that gives greater flexibility in recording and saving information.

Using whiteboards (or chalkboards) effectively

- Make sure that the board is clean.
- Use only whiteboard markers (not large textas) when writing on the board.
- Use a clean cloth or eraser for cleaning the board.
- Practise writing in a straight line with letters about 6–7 cm high.
- Write in lower case rather than capitals, as lower-case letters are easier to read.
- Write key points only.
- Avoid using the bottom half of the board as it difficult for people to see.
- Do not talk when facing the board; always turn round to face your audience when speaking.
- Always carry spare markers and erasers with you as a safeguard.
- If doing specific graphics, arrive early to practise them so that you can effectively use the board to the best advantage.
- Arrive early to check the equipment.

Using butcher's paper effectively

Butcher's paper comes in a large pad and is very useful for workshop presentations, as completed pages can be torn off and placed around the room for workshop members to add to or contemplate. It is the best way to collect considerable amounts of data.

- Practise writing in a straight line with letters about 6–7 cm high.
- Ask people in the group to write up information for you in a workshop as this will free you up to lead the group.
- Write in lower case rather than capitals as lower-case letters are easier to read.
- Write key points only.
- Use different coloured pens for different ideas, concepts, group responses or topics.
- Do not talk when writing. Always turn round to face your audience when speaking.
- Always carry spare pens with you as a safeguard.
- If doing specific graphics, arrive early to practise them so that you can effectively use the paper to the best advantage.
- Arrive early to check the equipment.

Audiovisual equipment can be daunting to any speaker but if you prepare ahead you can avoid most problems that you may encounter. Remember, it is vitally important to arrive early and check the equipment or talk with the audiovisual technician. Become acquainted with the equipment. Check it out and recheck it so that you are comfortable. Always carry a 'safety net' whether it is a duplicated disk with a set of overhead transparencies or extra whiteboard markers and erasers. Key to it all, always have a hard copy of your presentation in case all else fails. Preparation and more preparation, both before and at the event, will give you the confidence to perform, apparently seamlessly.

STEP 10

BE PROFESSIONAL

Greatness consists in trying to be great. There is no other way.

ALBERT CAMUS, *French playwright and novelist, 1913–1960*

Learn about the why and how of becoming more professional in all your speaking opportunities.

In the previous chapters you have learned how to create a speech, how to deliver it and how to 'do it your way'. You have gained knowledge of how to manage stage fright, cope with audiovisual equipment and achieve the perfect voice. Here is the final step that will allow you to become, not only a successful speaker, but someone who leaves a distinct imprint of your unique value as a speaker on all with whom you associate.

The reason I have included a chapter dedicated to being a professional is because of my twenty years of experience working with speakers of all calibres and profiles. Many speakers do not understand the importance of developing a well thought-of reputation. As Marlene Vaughan said, 'In public speaking, voice production is a total body experience'. Similarly, an audience's total experience of the speaker, gleaned from their attitude, energy, appearance and characteristics will, more often than not, affect their response to the speech.

William Faulkner, the Nobel prize winning novelist, said about writing novels: 'It takes ninety-nine per cent talent, ninety-nine per cent discipline, ninety-nine per cent work. He must never ever be satisfied with what he does. It never is as good as it can be done. Always dream and shoot higher than you know you can do.'

According to the *Macquarie Dictionary* (third edition), 'professional' means 'following an occupation as a means of livelihood or for gain'. That classic definition of 'professional' can be broadened to include everyone who undertakes a task or responsibility, not just those who are gainfully employed. For me, a 'professional' is an individual who takes a disciplined approach to all his or her actions. They are always willing to look at things differently, are considerate of others and are always asking 'What do I need to do to improve my performance?'

You may wish to pursue public speaking as a career. There are great opportunities for professional speakers of merit to make their contribution and earn a very satisfactory living from speaking out. If you are set on this course you will know what it takes to succeed in this arena and will no doubt be ahead of my text and into the next book, seminar or personal coaching that you think will help you achieve your goals.

Alternatively, standing on your feet and giving a presentation may be an important part of your day-to-day work. You realise that the better you can present, the more opportunities will come your way. People who speak with conviction and authority are seen as leaders. Speaking well is an essential tool in marketing yourself to others. You may be the individual who speaks infrequently and does not have ambitions to take it further, but believes wholeheartedly that, once you have learned a skill, it does not stop there, you go on to sharpen and hone it until it gleams.

I have a friend who teaches yoga. When she started yoga many years ago it was simply as an exercise to work off the stress that her senior management position in a world-renowned gallery demanded. As the years passed, she gained so much from her yoga practice that she hungrily read all she could about yoga techniques, practised regularly and took many additional workshops to supplement her knowledge. She even travelled to remote parts of Thailand to live in a hill-tribe village to study the subtleties of traditional Thai massage and to integrate its therapies into a Western approach to yoga.

When she retired, she moved from California to Kauai in the Hawaiian islands where she started to look for a suitable teacher with whom to continue her yoga practice and studies. At the time there was nothing to suit her needs and so she started practising on her own and found there were many friends who wanted to join her and asked her to lead a class. It was obvious to all who knew her that she would make a perfect teacher as she was continually striving to improve her own yoga practice and knowledge. As she had sought to improve herself she was now ready to share this talent with others. Her classes are always full and yoga devotees from around the world regard her highly.

She is always seeking to improve her knowledge, searching for more ways in which yoga can both help and heal the body, different ways in which to sequence the poses in order to achieve specific results, always with the thought of how she could help her students more effectively. To me she is the epitome of a professional.

CELEBRITY TIP

Creating a speech is a lot like creating a yoga class. It needs a beginning, or opening, which will relax and at the same time prepare students for what's to come, give some gentle exploratory movements etc. Next the body of the class can be strong and challenging or can be a softer and more mystical experience. Finally a closing, some decompression, calming poses and final relaxation and meditation. I do throw in some humour and – oh – just the right music and 'Bob's your uncle' – a memorable experience ...

PATRICIA HOWARD

My friend and colleague Lyndey Milan (food director of *The Australian Women's Weekly* and co-host of *Fresh*) has a short and pithy creed that she lives and works by: 'I don't do ordinary'. In a relatively short time I have seen her reach pinnacles in her career because she is always questing for excellence. Conversely, I know many 'professional' celebrities or performers who do not measure up to being a fully-fledged professional. They may enjoy the limelight but fail when it comes to the finer points, relying on their profile to carry them.

Becoming professional is not just for those who make a living from speaking; it is a desirable goal for everyone who has to speak on a frequent basis. For you it might mean a career promotion, for someone else it may be the feeling of true achievement in promoting a cause successfully to their target audience. The primary benefit of taking a more professional approach is that it increases your confidence and self-image. In other words, it encourages self-development. Wouldn't you like to be the best that you can, to achieve your highest potential?

To become a true professional you must ask yourself how would such a person behave. When you have identified those characteristics you can then start modelling the behaviour.

What are the characteristics of a professional? I think the attributes shown below are the key to developing a professional approach:

Self-development

- A true professional understands the importance of self-development.

  To succeed you need to keep personal gremlins at bay. Like all of us, professionals suffer from internal inadequacy mantras that taint their belief systems. They know that these negative messages are extremely powerful and that they can severely block them from reaching their full potential.

  Strive to control your mind; feed yourself with positive information so that the gremlins have less room to play. Edit your thoughts so that when you start to think negatively you can replace these negative thoughts with positive, affirming ideas such as: 'I believe in myself', 'I am a fine speaker', 'My presentation or speech is a winner', 'I am a person of integrity', 'I speak clearly and succinctly'. Focus on these affirmations as you repeat and absorb them. Although you may not believe these simplistic statements when you first start, gradually you begin to absorb the positive messages until these affirmations become an integral part of your self-image.

  The importance of positive affirmations was not lost on World Champion boxer Muhammad Ali. After he became Heavyweight Boxing Champion of the World for the third time he said: 'I am the greatest. I said that before I knew I was'.

- Instead of 'an apple a day to keep the doctor at bay', three times a day tell yourself all your key assets of talent and character. Write them down on a card that you can pull out at any stage of the day when you might be feeling a little down so that you can read them again and again.

- Focus on the now. Learn the virtue of concentrating, pulling your mind back to the present moment to savour, enjoy and experience it fully.
- Be kind to yourself – set realistic, achievable goals. Look for ways to manage your time more effectively. Exercise regularly. Eat healthy foods 85 per cent of the time.
- Recognise that every experience brings a blessing. Understand that we learn more from failure than from winning. Learn what not to do again. Learn how to handle disappointment. Learn how to handle rejection.
- Grow.

Integrity
- Being professional means looking for quality information rather than spurious gossip. Double-check your facts and data to make sure that these are always credible – by doing this your confidence and self-belief will increase.
- Carefully review all invitations and briefs to speak at functions. Don't put yourself in a situation where your integrity is compromised by lack of conviction for the subject or organisation, however tempting the offer may be.
- Understand the importance of building a good reputation. Return phone calls and reply to mail messages promptly. Submit your speech papers on time, if not before the due date. Follow up after the event to thank the organisers and ask for audience feedback.
- In short, make your word your bond.

Consistency
Dr Rosemary Stanton, one of Australia's most respected nutritionists, once said about healthy eating: 'It is what you do 85 per cent of the time that is important'. The same standards apply to the true professional. A major part of their time is given to a consistent approach to speech craft.

- Keep a notebook handy to jot down ideas or useful pieces of information that you may come across and can be added to your knowledge. Record anecdotal stories that you hear or read for possible use in the future.
- Search widely for the right resource material. None of the research that a speaker does is ever wasted. It increases your knowledge of the topic. Read copiously about your chosen subject, search the Internet and ask questions of others, always trying to expand your knowledge.
- Recognise that action drives inspiration.
- Don't begrudge editing your work, as judicious pruning will take your presentation from the ordinary into full bloom.
- Give yourself plenty of time to rehearse the presentation until you have it to the 'second skin' stage.
- Start early in the piece to manage your stage fears by practising visualisation and other techniques and create the opportunity for yourself to excel.

Dealing with criticism

As the author of the classic *The Power of Positive Thinking* Norman Vincent Peale said, 'The trouble with most of us is that we would rather be ruined by praise than saved by criticism'. A true professional will welcome anything that is going to help them give a better presentation even if it is painful at first.

- Ask for the opinions of others, as well as critiquing your own performance with a view to improving every nuance, shift of the head, hand gesture, every phrase and pronunciation of every word.
- Be hungry for self-improvement. A beige cardigan, while warm and eminently serviceable, will just not do; seek out that coat of many colours.
- Although you might smart and lick your wounds for a couple days after a critic has hit the mark, once you are

past this blow to your ego, gratefully assimilate the recommendations.

Managing the ego

A healthy ego is good but an ego on heat is not a pretty sight. It is lustful and demanding. The true professional keeps their ego on a leash. As a professional, recognise that you are not the only ego on the stage. Don't upstage other performers. Don't exploit your audience. Show respect to your fellow speakers and always remember to encourage or acknowledge the performances of others.

- Care about your audience. Do your research so that you will not offend or patronise your listeners. Be grateful to the audience for being there and tell them so with warmth, smiles and body language. Take delight in flirting with the audience. Respect each individual and realise that it is your job to try to win them over. Stand by John F. Kennedy's creed of 'what can I give' rather than what can they give me.

- Be courteous and respectful to everyone you work with. This courtesy and respect will be given back to you three-fold to ease your path.

- As a true professional strive to do it better each and every time.

- Consider how your presentation could be further enriched by fleshing out more of the argument, strengthening your word pictures with a metaphor, simile or the perfect cliché, illustrating a point more firmly, or injecting gentle humour to lighten the mood and ease the listener.

- Tape your voice and listen to it as objectively as you can. Listen for jarring nasal tones or rising inflections. Where you can rectify problem areas do so. If these problems are outside your influence or capabilities, seek counsel from other experts. Join a speaking club to practise your craft on a regular basis. Avail yourself of any classes or seminars that will give you greater knowledge and skills. This will give you that edge that will change you from a good speaker into a memorable speaker.

Time management

- Being professional means always being early or on time. No excuses about traffic conditions – take account of these before starting out.
- For your own peace of mind you need to arrive fresh, not stressed from running late. Use any extra time to check all that you need. This also gives you an opportunity to talk with some of the audience before you start.
- If you are late because of a factor beyond your control, let the organiser know in plenty of time so that your session can be rescheduled for later in the day or the next day.
- If you have to drop out because of illness or another catastrophe, give as much notice as possible and offer the name of an alternative speaker who could fill your place.
- Recognise that the organisers have put time and effort into planning any program so that it maintains the audience's interest and comfort. Understand the consequences to the program if a speaker runs over time.
- The audience anticipate that the allocated time will be adhered to. A speaker who does that gains their respect.
- Timing your speech begins right back at the preparation stage when you have got your speech or presentation to rehearsal stage.

Having worked with so many speakers over the past twenty years, I know conclusively that adopting a professional way of conducting yourself will pay dividends for any speaker.

Speakers who are 'professional' communicate better, relate better and are definitely more popular with audiences and organisers. People's response to you is intrinsic to how you view yourself. By modelling yourself on professionally minded people and practising their good habits and behaviours, your confidence and ability will grow. As a speaker you should always be looking for more knowledge and in the second part of this book you can find more in-depth information on specific speaking challenges.

PART 2

HANDLING SPECIFIC SPEAKING ASSIGNMENTS
with Confidence

THE
TOAST

Here's to us that are here, to you that are there, and the rest of us everywhere.

RUDYARD KIPLING, *novelist and poet, 1865–1936*

Find out how to propose a toast, whether it is the loyal toast, a toast to the bride and groom, or a celebration toast.

The tradition of drinking a toast began long ago when early Romans drank to their gods as part of their religious rites and as a mark of respect to the dead at ceremonial banquets. The ritual of raising their wine cup to salute others continued on down through history. The term 'toast' originated in Britain in Stuart times in the seventeenth century. It stemmed from the practice of putting a piece of toast in the bottom of the wine cup to improve the flavour of the wine. The toast started off as a salute to the health of the recipient. Today, as we raise our glasses, our good wishes are not limited to good health but may encompass wishes for happiness, success, safe journey, achievement and wealth.

Toasting is an important ritual at functions and formal occasions and as such needs to pay respect to traditions and protocol. Different cultures place great significance on correct protocol or the right etiquette of toasting. The more formal the occasion, the more attention should be given to protocol.

> *Toasting is an important ritual at functions and formal occasions and as such needs to pay respect to traditions and protocol.*

When giving a toast you should stand with your glass in hand. Preferably the glass should contain either an alcoholic or non-alcoholic drink. (There are some who believe that you should not use plain water for a toast.) The wording of the toast should be succinct (although this may depend on the occasion) and conclude with the invitation for all to stand and raise their glasses. The person being toasted should remain seated throughout the toast; they may nod their head or lift their glass in acknowledgement but etiquette dictates that they refrain from drinking their own toast.

Giving toasts is a popular pastime the world over, and many witty and eloquent words have been threaded together to create memorable toasts. The Irish, with their 'kiss of the Blarney stone', have created some memorable romantic and poetic toasts.

> *May the road rise to meet you,*
> *May the wind be always at your back,*
> *May the sun shine warm upon your face.*
> *And rains fall soft upon your fields.*
> *And until we meet again.*
> *May God hold you in the hollow of His hand.*

May your glass be ever full.
May the roof over your head be always strong.
And may you be in heaven
Half an hour before the devil knows you're dead.

Here's to you and yours
And to mine and ours.
And if mine and ours
Ever come across you and yours,
I hope you and yours will do
As much for mine and ours
As mine and ours have done
For you and yours.

The angels protect you,
And heaven accept you.
May the Irish hills caress you.
May her lakes and rivers bless you.
May the luck of the Irish enfold you.
May the blessings of Saint Patrick behold you.

May the Lord keep you in His hand
And never close His fist too tight.

The loyal toast

The loyal toast is a salutation given to the host country and its sovereign and is normally given at formal occasions. This toast is given either at the end of the meal or at the end of one course during the meal. Officially no smoking is allowed until after the loyal toast. Glasses should be filled and the master of ceremonies (emcee) should introduce the person who will give the toast.

- If the gathering is small, stand where you are seated and speak clearly and loudly so that everyone can hear.

- If it is a large gathering and you will have difficulty in being heard, move to the microphone with your glass and propose the toast from the lectern. Remain standing while the toast is being honoured.
- For most formal functions the loyal toast is straightforward. The correct protocol for Australia at this time in our history is: 'Ladies and gentlemen, please join me in the Loyal Toast – Her Majesty, the Queen of Australia'. Or you may prefer to say: 'Ladies and gentlemen, please join me in the toast to the Queen and people of Australia'.

If you are asked to propose a toast to a visiting dignitary, you can expect to be fully briefed by the organiser regarding the correct protocol and whether you will need to provide more than the simple 'Please raise your glasses' phrase.

Wedding speeches and toasts

During our lifetime many of us have to make a toast at a wedding. The traditional customs of only the bride's father, the groom and the best man making speeches are no longer *de rigeur* in modern weddings. The scope of family and friends who can play a role has broadened considerably. The material below will give you specific information and guidelines on traditional wedding toasts which can be adapted to suit most needs.

The bride's representative's speech

Weddings are all about rituals handed down from pagan times. Way back then, if a man saw someone who took his fancy he did not wait around for an introduction; helped by his best mate, he captured the fair maiden, literally, tethering her at the wrists and throwing some sort of smelly covering over her before taking her off to his lair. Today the bridal veil represents the covering and the gold ring on the bride's finger has its origins in the rope bindings that encircled her wrists.

In the more recent past, and still today in some cultures, the bride's parents gave a dowry to secure her future with the husband, who in turn was supposed to provide for her and any children. As the tradition evolved, the provision of a dowry in Western society changed into the bride's parents funding and hosting the wedding. Although this is not necessarily the case today, many wedding agendas keep the custom of the bride's father welcoming the guests and thanking everyone for coming, before moving on to propose the toast to the bride and groom.

If you are the father of the bride or you have been asked to propose the toast to the bride and groom, you will need to consider some of the following:

- Work out with the bride and groom how long they want you to speak and tailor your speech to suit.
- The success of this speech is all about balancing sincerity and humour. Your speech should express the depth of happiness and pride but also be light enough for the occasion. Sincerity, gratitude and nostalgia are the main ingredients, with plenty of humour to bind the mix. At a wedding everyone is happy and a speech with even the sloppiest attempt at humour will please the audience. The same rules apply as with all speech-making: be true to yourself and use language that you are comfortable with. If you use somebody else's material, personalise it until it suits your style of speaking and delivery.
- The introduction should welcome the guests, first mentioning the groom's parents and then welcoming all family members and friends. Special mention should be made if any guests have travelled from overseas or from a fair distance away to be at the wedding. At this stage you can also thank everyone who needs to be recognised, such as the aunties who did the flowers and the cake, and so on. The welcome and thanks should be short and gracious, leaving you more time to spend on the body of the speech.

- As you go into the body of your speech, talk about the bride. Obviously this is a memorable rite of passage for you both and as such it is your opportunity to say how beautiful she is, how proud you are, and speak about her journey from childhood to young womanhood. Personalise this section – put it into your own style and use some humour. The benchmark here is that the bride should understand clearly that her father is giving her away with love and pride. Humour is always welcome, but remember, sometimes edgy humour can muddy the waters of sincerity. It is better that you miss out on a laugh rather than fail to touch your daughter's heart. Let your heart do the talking; let your head do the reminiscing that will paint a picture of your daughter as you know her.

- The next step is to welcome the groom into your family. Touch on the good character of the groom. Anecdotal material is very useful here as it can give the audience a glimpse of the goodwill that you have for him. Use humour by all means but make it self-deprecating rather than at the groom's expense.

- Now focus on the bridal couple and offer some words of wisdom or advice on married life. While sincere homilies can suit, it will be more effective if it is funny. This humour can be home-grown or anecdotal, a joke or one-liner that you have researched. You can find some good joke books in the local library or appropriate one-liners from the Internet. Here are a few examples sourced from the Internet.

A man who gives in when he is wrong is a wise man.
A man who gives in when he is right is married.

Before marriage, a man will lie awake all night thinking about something you say. After marriage he will fall asleep before you finish.

Marriage is when a man and woman become as one.
The trouble starts when they try to decide which one.

- Conclude your speech with the formal toast: 'Ladies and gentlemen, family and friends, please join me in toasting the bride and groom'.

The groom or bride's speech

As recipients of the toast to the bride and groom, it is customary for the groom to reply on behalf of his bride. Today, however, our social customs are changing rapidly and many brides prefer to take a more active part in the reception proceedings, so the bride may elect to answer or the couple may decide to do this jointly. The speaker(s) should consider the following:

- Allocate the timing for this speech when planning the reception. If the wedding is a sit-down 'do', then this speech should always be made between courses. Service should stop during the speeches. You will need to consider the best time for this, as the best man needs to speak before you cut the cake and move into the other activities.
- This speech should lean towards sincerity rather than humour. This is the time to do some serious thanking of supportive family members and friends. It is also time to give a public declaration of the love you feel for your new partner.
- In the introduction of your speech express your thanks to the parents of the bride, especially if the wedding has run along traditional lines with the bride's parents hosting the wedding reception. The groom should not only thank them for their support but also for the gift of their daughter. The groom should also thank his own parents for their support.
- Next is the moment the guests are all waiting for, the time for you to wax lyrically about your new bride or groom. This should definitely be 'oohs and ahs' territory. It may be

that you have written your own vows and these have expressed this love in the preceding ceremony. If so, you might reiterate part of these or expand on them slightly. While this is you and your partner's moment, remember the guests and keep it reasonably short, although of course totally romantic.

- Once you have paid homage to your partner, it is time to move back into expressing your gratitude to the guests for their kind wishes and presents. Then thank all the wedding attendants, the flowergirls, page boys, ring bearers, ushers, and groomsmen. As you thank the best man it is the groom's opportunity to give the best man a bit of a serve before he speaks – because undoubtedly he has plenty in store for you.
- Following on, acknowledge and thank the bridesmaids, touching on the support they have given the bride and complimenting them on their appearance. Finally propose the toast to the bridesmaids by saying: 'Ladies and gentlemen, please join me in toasting the bridesmaids'.

The best man's reply on behalf of the bridesmaids

Traditionally the best man's speech is the last speech in a formal wedding agenda. The audience anticipate this speech eagerly and have grown to accept this as the fun and slightly risqué end of proceedings. By the time the party reaches the best man's speech they are feeling very well indeed, love and goodwill are flowing, and now they are ready to play. So the best man's role is to be jester to the wedding court and fulfil their expectations. If you are best man, consider the following:

- You will need to work out the timing of your speech with the bride and groom. Timing plays a vital role in the proceedings as the venue may only provide a limited time. You will need to be aware that the cake still has to be cut, the garter removed, the bouquet thrown and the wedding waltz to be waltzed and that is before you even get to the dance floor!

- While it is expected that your speech will 'roast' rather than toast the groom, it should be clean enough for the elderly relatives in the audience. It is a matter of finding the right balance between risqué and vulgar. Always err on the side of the slightly risqué. Leave the audience wanting more, rather than wishing you would disappear.

- The introduction should be sincere and reasonably serious. Reply immediately to the toast that has been offered to the bridesmaids. Thank the bride on their behalf. Then move straight into expressing your good wishes for the bride and groom's future together. It is suitable here to talk sincerely about the bride and how happy the groom has been since they met. Relate some happy incidents of the romance.

- As you move into the main body of your speech, thank the groom for asking you to be best man. Now is 'roast' time. Your job is to embarrass the groom in a goodhearted way. Themes about the groom's characteristics are always a good way to introduce humour. Mind mapping all the groom's idiosyncrasies will definitely make this task easier.

  Humour is made up of various elements – a sense of the ludicrous, a play on words or unexpected twists in the story, heavy-handed exaggeration, all delivered with a straight face and the measured use of the pause. You may be able to enlist the help of the ushers in creating your speech. Props can also be useful in adding texture and dimension. You can choose to weave the congratulatory messages into the beginning of this part of the speech with a clever 'bogus' fax creating a springboard for the 'roast'.

  However, it is important to remember that while the stag night offered you a great opportunity to talk about the groom's romantic liaisons, the wedding is definitely not the place to talk about the groom's conquests or the bride's, for that matter. Remember also to pay appropriate respect to those who have sent messages and best wishes.

- As you bring the speech to a conclusion, swing the mood pendulum back to sincerity and thank the hosts on behalf of the guests.

Congratulatory and other celebration toasts

Congratulatory and celebration party toasts may include the retirement of a co-worker, a move to a new city or country, a coming of age, a wedding, a milestone birthday, a christening, a graduation, an anniversary, or any other rite of passage. The Irish toasts featured earlier are great for informal gatherings where the warmth of the company and a drop or two of wine tend to make you want to toast the world at large, but for formal parties and functions, a congratulatory or celebratory toast requires a little more work. Always view a celebration toast as a speech.

This type of speech should be light in nature and focus on the recipient's characteristics. It always benefits from the use of humour. It does not have to be Comedy Store quality as, by the time you deliver it, the goodwill of the guests will be at a peak and they will be prepared to laugh at even the merest hint of humour.

Here are some general rules that apply to each of these speeches.

- The timing of the speech should be suited to the style of party. If it is formal you will need to find out how long you are expected to speak; if it is an informal gathering the timing may not be so crucial but a good rule of thumb is that toasts should not drag on. If you cannot say it in three to four minutes maximum, then it may be too long for guests to absorb.
- Research is important – you need to find out all that you can about the person. Even if you are close to them, there are always certain things that you have forgotten or need

clarification about or may get a different perspective about when talking to another family member or friend.

- Mind mapping is the best tool for creating this speech. The best material is anecdotal and suitable funny quotes will add to the richness of your prose.
- The content of your speech should always focus on the purpose of the celebration. This is a time to speak positively about the person's life, achievements and character.
- A congratulatory toast needs to convey the goodwill and congratulations of all the guests, so be sensitive to any special issues that will be touched on.
- It is a time for lightness and humour. Depending on the occasion and definitely depending on the recipient, it can be seen as an opportunity to gently roast the star of the show. But be very careful here, as some people at the centre of attention could absolutely hate this. If this is the case, make sure all matters in the speech about them are warm and fuzzy and make the humorous element self-deprecating.
- The conclusion of the speech is where you ask people to raise their glasses and join you in the toast. Some examples for different toasts are given below to point you in the right direction. Add to them or discard them; use your own words to create a toast that is appropriate the toastee.

Toasts for specific occasions

Retirement of a co-worker
Ladies and gentlemen, family and friends, please join me in wishing _____ a happy and fulfilling retirement.

Move to a new city or country
Ladies and gentlemen, family and friends, please join me in wishing _____ bon voyage and a successful new

start that brings happiness and rewards beyond his/her/their expectations.

Coming of age
Ladies and gentlemen, family and friends, please join me in wishing _____ a very happy birthday and a life full of joy and success.

Milestone birthday
Ladies and gentlemen, family and friends, please join me in wishing _____ good health, long life and happiness.

Christening
Ladies and gentlemen, family and friends, please join me in wishing baby _____ a healthy, happy, fulfilling and long life.

Graduation
Ladies and gentlemen, family and friends, please join me in congratulating _____ and wishing him/her every success in his/her chosen career.

Anniversary
Ladies and gentlemen, family and friends, please join me in wishing _____ the enjoyment of many more years of mutual love and companionship.

AN EXPRESSION OF THANKS

What really flatters a man is that you think him worth flattering.

GEORGE BERNARD SHAW, *John Bull's Other Island*

Learn how to give a simple expression of thanks or a more formal vote of thanks.

A vote of thanks speech was my first 'stand up and be counted' speech in public. I was a brand new member of the Women's Institute in a small village in the Midlands in the UK at the time. Yes, the chapter I was involved in for twelve months was very reminiscent of the film *Calendar Girls*, but fortunately I was fully clothed when I gave the speech. It was a steep learning curve for me as I had no time to prepare. The person who was to have given the thanks fainted in the middle of the meeting and as I was sitting within reach of the program organiser I was asked to stand in. Unfortunately I had not learned to form the word 'No' at that stage, which was a pity because the speaker had been rather boring. I had switched off and was mentally working on domestic matters. As you can imagine, it was the shortest and probably the most ineffective vote of thanks on record. Still, you learn more from failure than from success, and it made me aware of the importance of this 'seemingly' simple type of speech.

Both the simple expression of thanks and the more formal vote of thanks are speeches that express gratitude for a job well done, whether it is to a speaker or other worthy recipient. The primary object of these speeches is to represent the body of the audience in showing appreciation of effort. If you are the person giving the thanks, remember that the recipient should still be centre stage in the audience's mind. You are merely a conduit for expressing the collective gratitude of the audience or meeting.

The speech should be short and totally relevant to the recipient's contribution. It is desirable to touch on highlights of the speech or work they have given, but it should in no way be a critique or evaluation of the endeavour. Those being thanked should always go away with the firm knowledge that their contribution was valued.

Normally this style of speech is light in nature and benefits from the use of humour, but the degree of levity or seriousness will depend on the situation. Most importantly, whether the thanks are lighter in nature or demand a more serious approach, the speech should always be delivered with grace and sincerity.

Don't be fooled into thinking that this style of speech is simple; it requires a certain skill to be effective. Too many or a list of tributes is not good. If you want to avoid the cringe factor, don't go over the top with the accolades. Let common sense guide your choice of compliments so that sincerity can shine through.

This is the time for the speaker's ego to be on a leash, a time for appropriate 'humility', defined by the *Macquarie Dictionary* (third edition) as a 'quality of being humble, a modest sense of one's own significance'. No Uriah Heep posturing, just a clean, simple appreciation that completely spotlights the recipient.

The same rules apply as those for preparing any speech – find out what is expected of you by the organiser, whether it is a formal or informal vote of thanks, research your audience and prepare as much as you can ahead of time. It will help to know the speaker or group's background. If you have been asked to give thanks to a speaker, listen closely and, where possible, take note of highlights that capture your and/or the audience's attention. Although you are speaking on behalf of the audience, your style of speech will obviously be subjective. It will be pleasing to the speaker to know that you have been paying close attention and that you particularly enjoyed or endorsed certain ideas, concepts or phrases that they used.

If you are thanking an individual or a group of people for the work they have undertaken, make sure that you cover all aspects of their contribution. Often, for many people who give time and energy generously to a cause, this is the only occasion on which they will be recognised officially. Try to make it as personal and as pertinent as possible so you can connect with them sincerely. For most, the work they do is a labour of love, which they contribute willingly and tirelessly. You have a chance to make them feel very special.

For an expression of thanks simply conclude by asking the audience to join you in showing their appreciation.

If you have been asked to give a more formal vote of thanks, which is to be documented in the minutes of a meeting, approach this in a more conventional manner. A vote of thanks in these terms should be viewed as a motion that must be put to the meeting through the medium of the chairperson or Chair. As the 'mover' of the motion of a vote of thanks, you must address the Chair before moving into the words of commendation. It is always the correct protocol to acknowledge the Chair first. For example, 'Mr Chairman/Madam Chair, I have much pleasure in moving a vote of thanks to _____ for ...'; then proceed to the body of your speech.

The correct formality at the conclusion of the speech is for the Chair to 'put the question' – 'You have heard the motion. I ask the meeting to carry it with acclamation'. As you start your concluding remarks they need to strongly signal, either by words or voice variation, that you are about to finish so that the Chair can continue.

Many clubs and associations do not bother with the finer points of correct meeting rules and prefer a less conformist approach to their proceedings. While it is not correct protocol, they may prefer you as the mover of the motion to conclude with the words 'It gives me great pleasure to move this vote of thanks, please carry it in the usual way, by acclamation. If you are not familiar with the club or organisation's traditions, always check beforehand so that you are prepared and comfortable in using either method of conclusion.

A seconder for this formal motion is not really necessary and will only protract proceedings unnecessarily. But again, this will depend on the club or association's customs. The use of a seconder for such a motion is rare, but if you have been asked to second the motion, make sure your words are short and sweet. Acknowledge that 'It gives you pleasure to second the motion', and then express your appreciation in a couple of sentences. Try to avoid repeating what the mover of the motion has said. Add a fresh sweetener to the melting pot of thanks.

Very occasionally a speech or speaker does not gel and you cannot identify any apparent highlights to weave into your speech of thanks. While this is a difficult situation, you can always find some magic if you look hard enough. Maybe the opinion of the speaker differs from the views of the audience. In that case, thank them for bringing a different perspective and giving all present cause to think through their position. Maybe the speech is simply not your style or in your opinion went nowhere, but you or the audience warmed to their commitment, personality or courage. Look at these characteristics and build them into your speech. If all else fails, you can always stretch the thanks for the person's efforts, time and energy.

It is always good to have a short pithy quotation to fall back on, whether the speech is brilliant or otherwise, and I recommend you research a couple of relevant ones for the particular occasion that will fill the bill.

Here are some generic quotes that may be useful to thank a speaker or worker.

For a speaker
I can think of nothing more agreeable to the brain and the ear than a speech adorned and embellished with wise thoughts and fine language.

CICERO, *On the Orator, 55 BC*

Of all kinds of success, that of an orator is the most pleasing.

OLIVER GOLDSMITH, *The Bee, no. 7*

True eloquence consists in saying all that should be said, and that only.

DUC DE LA ROCHEFOUCAULD

Eloquence lies as much in the tone of the voice, in the eyes, and in the speaker's manner, as in his choice of words.

DUC DE LA ROCHEFOUCAULD

He is the best orator who can turn men's ears into eyes.

ARABIC PROVERB

For the worker or contributor
The only gift is a portion of thyself.

RALPH WALDO EMERSON

The best portion of a good man's life, is his little, nameless, unremembered acts of kindness and of love.

WILLIAM WORDSWORTH

Committee work is like a soft chair – easy to get into but hard to get out of.

KENNETH J. SHIVELY

Only the person who has faith in himself is able to be faithful to others.

ERIC FROMM

Many persons have a wrong idea of what constitutes true happiness. It is not attained through self-gratification but through fidelity to a worthy purpose.

HELEN KELLER

Each honest calling, each walk of life, has its own elite,
its own aristocracy based on excellence of performance.

JAMES BRYANT CONANT

Guidelines for an expression or vote of thanks

- If thanking a speaker, listen and take notes.
- If thanking a worker or a group, research their background and contribution beforehand.
- Make the thanks pertinent or relevant to the speech or contribution.
- Never critique.
- Don't be overly gushy.
- Be sincere and humble in the truest sense.
- Remember, the recipient should always be the focus of the speech.
- Where appropriate use humour to lighten the tone.
- If it is a formal vote of thanks, investigate the organisation's traditional manner of delivery.

The recipient should always be the focus of the expression-of-thanks speech.

MASTER OF CEREMONIES

The toastmaster introduced the speaker with great fervor, stressing her years of faithful service to the club and eulogizing her ability and charm. Somewhat overwhelmed, the speaker faced the audience. 'After such an introduction' she said disarmingly, 'I can hardly wait to hear what I've got to say.'

ADNELLE H. HESKETT, *Reader's Digest*

Understand the responsibilities of a master of ceremonies, including specific guidelines for the roles of Chair or emcee at a seminar or conference, a commentator in a masterclass and a wedding emcee. This chapter also provides valuable guidelines to help you become an effective and sensitive interviewer.

A master of ceremonies, toastmaster, anchorperson, compere, host or emcee (hereafter called the emcee) is the vital person who smooths the transition of one presentation to the next in a variety of formal functions and conferences. An emcee's expertise is much in demand for formal events such as conferences and seminars, weddings, launches, fashion and other trade shows, charity balls, fundraising dinners or lunches and any other occasion where speakers need to be introduced.

Characteristics of a good emcee

Star and funnyman Billy Crystal is probably a name that springs to mind when we think of the role of emcee. Billy is indisputably the American favourite to host the Oscar award ceremonies. Crystal says he physically trains for the job for weeks ahead. 'It's an endurance race,' he said. 'If my body doesn't feel right I don't feel good on stage.' Preparation and more preparation is the key to his presentation. 'We write thousands of jokes going in. It's like creating a football playbook with options.'

The role of an emcee is the key to the success of an event. Not all speakers are suited to this role, as it requires slightly different and additional skills compared to a regular speaker's presentation ability. As emcee you need to be creative and flexible enough to deal with any unexpected changes, hiccups or surprises that arise, even in the best-organised events. You will need the ability to think on the run and be able to turn a negative situation into a positive.

For example, at an awards ceremony, 100-year-old Hal Roach, the venerated Laurel & Hardy producer, was introduced while sitting in the audience. He stood up and chatted on without a mike for what seemed like several minutes. The television audience at home couldn't hear a word. This could have spelt disaster for the show but emcee Billy Crystal completely turned the situation around with his famous comeback: 'It seems appropriate that he got his start in silent films'.

Another major quality you need is the ability to empathise with fellow presenters. This is a role that requires you to nurture rather than to star, although you will star if you can successfully master the art of letting the other fellow be the star. If you do this well, you build the necessary tension and audience anticipation to warmly receive the next presentation. If you do it well, you make the speaker look and feel good, and this in turn gives an edge to their performance.

Here are some general guidelines to help you become a successful emcee.

Guidelines for an emcee

Prior to the event

- Meet with the organisers for a thorough briefing on the style of event, the make-up of the audience, the program, speakers and timing. Discuss the time needed for your welcoming comments and introductions to speakers, as this must be factored into the agenda. Request a database of speakers' contact details, as well as biographical profiles for each speaker.

- Verify with the organisers that they will be the only people authorised to give you changes or directions. Often when there is more than one master, communication can become fraught. Your job will be easier if you can establish this earlier rather later.

- As the event gets closer, request a detailed running sheet so that you know exactly what is happening and when. This running sheet should include all the program details, hospitality breaks, meal service and any specific audiovisual requirements of the speakers.

- Contact each of the speakers and confirm the titles of their presentations and their biographical details, as well as finding out how they prefer to be introduced. Often busy speakers will submit bios that are much too long and some inexperienced emcees can fall into the trap of reading everything. Edit their biographical details to suit.

While the event organisers will have written to the speakers giving them full details of the agenda, it is a good idea to remind them of the time allocated for their speech. Ask them if they would like some sort of signal when time is running short. Depending on the event, a bell is a useful warning device. If not, one of the organisers can sit in the audience and give an appropriate signal. It is important to be quite firm about timing, as the responsibility for the program running to time comes down to you. Advise the speaker that if they do go over time, you will certainly ring the bell again or give another signal; if they receive this second signal, they must close immediately.

Ask them about their special needs, particularly audiovisual ones (while this will have been arranged with the event organisers and is not your responsibility, it is useful for you to know). Are they confident with the audiovisual equipment they are going to use?

Remind them to arrive with plenty of time to find parking and time to relax, refresh and meet other key players.

- You will need to prepare your own running sheet or you may be able to adapt the organisers' running sheet for this purpose. You will also need to prepare a script or memory prompter notes which contain the following:
  - Opening comments. These should include a welcome to guests, a background to the function or conference, any housekeeping details, and an overview of the program. Investigate the correct protocol with the organiser.
  - An introduction for each speaker and the title of their presentation
  - A cache of additional pertinent material that can be used as a fall-back plan

- - Quotes or suitable comments that might fit into the program.
- Prepare as much as you can beforehand, including your concluding comments.
- Rehearse; practise your visualisations to feel confident.
- Make sure that you have all your material clearly sorted so that you know exactly where to access any particular information at any moment. The less obtrusive speakers' notes are more suitable for other speaking assignments, but as an emcee you need to be totally organised, not only for your time at the lectern, but to keep everyone else on track. I find the best method in this case is to place the material in chronological order in plastic sleeves in a ringbinder.
- Decide on the clothes you are going to wear. While your demeanour is focused on making other people look good, it is important for you to visually make an impact. The emcee role demands authority and your clothes should reflect this. Choose an outfit that makes a positive statement about you as a person.
- Make the organisers your best friends. They will be able to iron out any wrinkles and follow up on the speakers for you if you are having difficulty contacting them. Meet with the organisers immediately prior to the event. By then all the last-minute details will have fallen into place and they will be able to brief you on any changes. This is a good time to discuss the audiovisual arrangements and if there is anything specific you need to know and understand, or if you will be required to assist the speakers in any way.

At the event

- Arrive early to confirm all arrangements with the organisers. Investigate the venue in case you need to give directions in the housekeeping part of your opening comments. If there is an audiovisual technician present ask them to run through the equipment. If the occasion does not warrant the use of a technician, ask the organiser to brief you.

- Meet with speakers who may have arrived and run through their timing and any signals you have agreed on.

- Start the program on time. Keep a watch on the lectern as you speak. I find a digital watch preferable, as it is easier to read when speaking.

- Welcome the guests, using the right protocol for any dignitaries. Go through the housekeeping details, which should always include the request to turn off mobile phones. Move onto your opening comments and an overview of the program.

- Introduce the first speaker. Lead the applause as they come to the podium or lectern. Listen carefully to their speech. When the speaker finishes, return to the lectern and thank them and comment very briefly on their words. This should not be a critique of the speech but should highlight a positive angle. The role of emcee is to act as a host, so all your actions and words must be courteous.

- In your concluding statements include a summary of the proceedings. If you need to thank people who have contributed to the success of the event, now is the time to do this. Any other comments you feel you would like to make should be positive and leave the audience feeling glad that they have attended.

Guidelines for a seminar or conference Chair or emcee

The responsibilities associated with emceeing a seminar or conference can be onerous. The days are usually very full, and often there are multiple days, layered with dinners and other social activities. It will entail a considerable amount of work on your part. As well as the general guidelines for an emcee presented earlier, consider these additional items.

- Look at the organisers' demands on your time and assess whether these are physically and intellectually feasible. Holding an audience's attention over several hours in a day is very tiring, let alone over several days. If expectations are that you cover the entire conference and then are expected to host the gala dinner, it might make more sense to have more than one emcee. Choosing the emcee to fit the proceedings is beneficial for both the organisers and the audience. Different people shine in different ways – it is extremely difficult, I won't say impossible, 'being all things to all people all of the time'!

- Your preparation will be substantial and I suggest you work very closely with the organisers who can help you in this. You will still benefit from contacting every speaker yourself as it gives you the opportunity to build some necessary rapport. The chemistry between you at the conference will work better if you have taken time to get to know them a little. I find that if an emcee does not speak with the presenters beforehand, the introduction can be sterile and not as warm.

- With a full program where speakers come in throughout the day, you will obviously not be able to greet them all. This is where the organisers will step in and make sure you are aware of any problems, such as speakers running late.

- Arrive at the venue very early. You will need to spend time with the organisers and audiovisual technicians. Find out how to change the microphone height and how to use the remote control and laser pointer for a slide show, as well as arrange an overview of any other equipment the speakers may want to use. You do not have to be an expert but this knowledge can be valuable if a speaker has difficulties. Confirm any special timing signals for speakers so that the organisers can facilitate these. This is also a good time to synchronise running sheets.

- Time should be factored in to allow you to summarise speakers' presentations. This could be done at the end of a morning session or at the end of the day if the conference goes over more than one day. This will help the audience to see the bigger picture emerging.

- Your conclusion of the proceedings should be as the general guidelines suggest, but it may be appropriate to comment on the success or otherwise of the forum. Discuss this with the organisers and/or other authorities beforehand. If the goals of the conference have not been met, couch any negative conclusions in a positive 'way forward' framework.

- After the conference, write thank-you notes to the speakers and organisers for their contributions. Not only is this a polite gesture, it is a valuable public relations exercise.

Guidelines for a wedding emcee

Emceeing a wedding is an honour. It may be that you are a family member or close friend of the happy couple. As you do your planning, it is essential that you work closely with the bride and groom to achieve what they want from their day. Use the general emcee guidelines to help you prepare, as well as considering items like the ones below that are specific to this event.

- The role of a wedding emcee is slightly different in as much as it means you are the one who will introduce the reception activities, as well as the speeches.

- Decide with the bride and groom whether they want you to take the more formal role of toastmaster, where you stick strictly to an agreed script. This will probably mean you introduce, briefly and succinctly, the various elements and rituals that make up the wedding reception.

Or it can be approached in a more relaxed style – you still do the same tasks but you have more scope for fun and there is more opportunity for you to put your imprint on the event.

- If the bride and groom choose this second style, humour is most definitely appropriate at most weddings. Remember, though, that the best man traditionally has first go at this. Check with all the speakers and make sure you are not doubling up on material. If you are stuck for humorous quotes or one-liners, the Internet is a great resource to find wedding wit. (For further help, see After-Dinner or Humorous Speeches, pp. 231–243.)

- Any humour you use should be woven into the introductions or flow of proceedings. Make sure the humour is sensitive to all the bridal party guests. Risqué is acceptable to most people but avoid anything smutty. Do not mention previous relationships that either of the couple may have had. It is important to plan your linking comments and one-liners before the event.

The order of proceedings

Modern wedding ceremonies are changing and there is no one correct etiquette when it comes to the order of proceedings at the reception. Any proceedings should always centre on the wishes of the bride and groom.

A 'traditional' order of proceedings at the reception is given below that will be useful as a guide. However, the order of proceedings and any additional toasts, say to the parents of the bride and groom, should be based upon discussions with the bride and groom-to-be.

- Prepare your own running sheet with timing and try to stick to time as most wedding venues provide limited time for the reception.

- Ask someone to signal to you when the bride and groom are ready to join the reception. Announce the arrival of the bride and groom to the reception room. For example, 'Ladies and gentlemen, family and friends, be upstanding and welcome Mr and Mrs _____'.
- If grace is to be said before the meal, introduce the person doing this simply and respectfully, for example, 'Father John will now say grace', or 'The bride's cousin Jane Smith will now say grace'.
- When it comes to speech time, first introduce the father of the bride or the person who will offer the toast to the bride and groom.
- Introduce the groom or bride, or both of them, to reply to the toast and propose the toast to the bridesmaids.
- Introduce the best man to respond to the toast to the bridesmaids.
- Announce that the bride and groom will cut the cake.
- If there is to be dancing, the dancing should start with the bride and groom leading the bridal waltz. The other formalities to follow are the tossing of the bouquet and garter. Finally a circle is formed to farewell the bride and groom. If the reception is formal, it might be appropriate to announce these activities.

Guidelines for the masterclass emcee or commentator

A masterclass is a class that is given to talented students by an expert in a particular field. Today the scope of a masterclass has broadened to accommodate an audience of enthusiastic amateurs or interested observers. By definition a masterclass requires an expert or master of a skill to present this class. It is fitting that the emcee or professional commentator when hosting this class should have a sound knowledge of the subject involved.

Again, the general guidelines presented earlier will offer valuable guidance here. The following specific items should also help you with the intricacies of this type of assignment.

Prior to the event

- Obtain a thorough briefing from the organisers. This information should include a detailed breakdown of the audience and the objectives the organisers want to achieve from the class.
- Talk at length with the presenter to ascertain how they are going to structure and present the class.
- Will they need assistance with any of the activities?
- What do they personally want to achieve from the class?
- How do they like to be introduced to the group?
- Do they require any specific timing signals?
- What audiovisual equipment will they be using? Would they like you to help with this?

At the event

- Presenters sometimes find it difficult to talk and use their hands at the same time. It is your job to make sure that you fill in the gaps during these flat moments. You might use this time to recap on what the audience has seen to date or simply describe the activity taking place.
- If there are key points that you know the presenter wants to make, rephrase a statement to emphasise this to the audience.

If the masterclass consists of a panel of experts who have been asked to discuss a specific topic, there may be some slightly different aspects to consider.

Prior to the event

- Obtain a written brief from the organisers, that includes all the objectives that they want to achieve. The organisers may have drafted some questions that they believe will steer the discussions in the right direction but they will anticipate that you will use your discretion in guiding the discussion. It becomes your responsibility to elicit the information from the panel.

- Contact all the presenters to gain an understanding of the level of expertise they bring to the panel. Find out how they like to be introduced to the audience. Discuss with them the time limits of the session and ask them to be aware that you may have to cut their replies short if you are going to give all panel members equal time.

- When you have all the information about the panel members, review the draft questions and consider how effective they are going to be. Redraft them where necessary and consider additional lines of questioning in case things do not go according to plan.

At the event

- Make sure that the panel members have equal opportunity to make their point or present their viewpoint. More forceful panel members can override the quieter ones, so keep a tight rein on these speakers. The members of the panel have been chosen to bring an even-handed observation to the discussion and if you allow the more pushy ones to take over, the opportunity to give the audience a balanced view is reduced.

- Your concluding statements should contain a summary of the class, which means you need to listen intently. Have a pen and notepad with you, although it may not always be possible for you to take notes, as you should be conscious of what is happening and be ready to step in if needed.

Interviewer

The opportunity to conduct an interview publicly may not arise too frequently but, if it does, grab it with both hands, especially if you know that you have all the attributes of a caring emcee. A good interview is like a work of art – the ability to draw the best from a person must be the ultimate reward for an interviewer. Certainly any audience enjoys being a voyeur as the chemistry between the two people unfolds in front of them. You only have to consider the popularity of Michael Parkinson's television interviews that have endured over the years.

> *The most important skill for an interviewer is the ability to actually listen to the other person ... To listen means being present in the moment.*

The most important skill for an interviewer is the ability to actually listen to the other person. Listening is something that people do not always do well. Often their minds are three steps ahead, thinking of what they can say that will complement or top the communication of the speaker. To listen means being present in the moment and taking in the whole communication. It means using all your senses to understand what another person is saying.

The interviewer also needs to be compassionate and sensitive to the speaker. A good interviewer is unobtrusive. *Enough Rope with Andrew Denton* on ABC Television shows clearly the skill of a good interviewer. Andrew deftly brings an interviewee to where he wants them. His choice of words and manner, although edged with humour, are always courteous. When he explores an issue it is sensitively done and most of his subjects answer his questions even if the topic is sore or raw for them.

A poor interviewer is one who probes coarsely, opening up old and new wounds. Instead of listening and getting their cues from the person they are interviewing, they allow themselves to be led by the questions they have previously determined to ask, an autocue or a producer who is pushing for results. A good interviewer will set their own boundaries of integrity and respect for those whom they interview and will not be seduced into exploiting someone for the sake of a newsworthy story.

Good old Auntie does some things extremely well and *Australian Story* on ABC Television is an absolute model of 'less is more'. An interviewer does not even appear and yet we are aware that the story has skilfully been drawn out from the people involved. Although it is clear that the filming of each piece has been completed over a period of time and the producers have skilfully edited it to bring together the essence of the story, it is possible to see that a good interviewer will set the wheels in motion with relevant, careful questions, and then sit back and listen, prompting only when the subject slows or gets off track.

Here are some guidelines to consider when preparing an interview.

Guidelines for preparing an interview

- Research is critical for the success of the interview. Make sure, however, that the research is credible, as I have seen interviewers tripped with unreliable research.
- Find out if there are any 'no go' areas for the interviewee and honour these.
- Find out how they like to be introduced.
- Before the interview, talk to the person generally to develop a feeling of rapport. You need to put them at ease if the interview is going to be interesting.
- Spend some time going through what direction you would like to take with your questions and secure your inter-viewee's agreement.
- Ask open-ended, simple questions so that the subject can answer them easily.

- If the person is shy or reticent, suggest that the interview is purely a conversation between the two of you and that they should address their answers to you rather than to the audience or the camera.
- If the interview is being recorded or televised, give the interviewee an overview of what to expect during the filming.
- For the difficult interviewee, one who isn't going to talk in any detail or for any length of time, keep the questions rolling and never show your frustration or discomfort.
- Early on, as you do your research and prepare your questions, develop some mechanisms for coping with any problem areas you may face in the interview. You should locate sufficient material and questions to carry you through a reasonably unresponsive interview. Visualise the interview progressing, consider possible obstacles, but see yourself overcoming these with confidence and dignity.

Unless you are a celebrity emcee at a gala awards night, like Billy Crystal, you will often find an emcee's role is undervalued, but herein lies the essence of a good emcee's work. It is a question of setting the scene so that other speakers may star. The task is considerable, needing significant preparation, compassion and the ability to think on your feet. Some speakers will never make brilliant emcees but equally there are emcees who are profoundly better at orchestrating a speaker's program than making a speech. It is a question of knowing your limitations. Don't accept this role unless you know that you are content to let others shine.

EULOGY

His life was gentle and the elements so mixed in him that Nature might stand up and say to the world 'This was a man'.

WILLIAM SHAKESPEARE, *Julius Caesar*

This chapter will give you the wherewithal to present this stressful speech.

Dr Elisabeth Kubler-Ross, a psychiatrist who spent much of her life working with the dying, was one of the world's most respected authorities on grief. She identified five stages of grief that people go through following the loss of a loved one. In her book, *On Death and Dying*, she named these stages as denial and isolation, anger, bargaining, depression and finally acceptance. These feelings are a necessary part of the healing process. Often our society wants to put a time limit on others' grief and the bereaved feel pressured into putting on a 'brave face'. By denying these feelings they take longer to heal.

Bereavement experts tell us a meaningful funeral helps us to deal with the loss of a loved one. It helps us face the reality of the death and provides a focus that enables us to express our united grief. Western society tends to be embarrassed about displays of grief. Grieving is a natural part of life and the funeral ritual allows us the opportunity to cry and vent our anguish. The eulogy is pivotal in the funeral ceremony; it is a testimony to a person who is loved and mourned by the gathering of family and friends.

The *Macquarie Dictionary* defines eulogy as a 'speech or writing in praise of a person or thing, especially a set oration in honour of a deceased person'. But a eulogy is not only the last public hurrah to a loved one; it plays a vital role in the grieving process, allowing mourners to focus on their loss and grieve openly, as well as prompting their individual memories of the person. It starts the process of saying farewell and the realisation that this beloved person is no more and will now become a memory. In short, it is the beginning of the journey of healing.

I am sure you have been to a funeral where the eulogiser may not have known the person and that lack of genuine knowledge is obvious. It is almost as if they are speaking of someone completely different from your viewpoint. It seems that they didn't even know them.

A good eulogy will trace, with love and gratitude, all those aspects of a life, imperceptible warts and all. Family and friends will take comfort from a ceremony that manages to capture the essence of the person.

To give a eulogy at a funeral or memorial is a unique and special honour, not to be entered into lightly or vainly. It can be flattering to be asked to give such a privileged oration but before deciding you must make sure you are the right person for the task. You must be confident that you can be sensitive enough to represent all those closest to the deceased, either family or friends. Often it is too difficult for very close members of the family to present the eulogy and someone close to the family may be able to do this more objectively.

You must have sufficient time to do it effectively. It will take time to talk with family and friends and gather the necessary material. You must have reasonable confidence that you will have sufficient control over your own emotions to carry it through with dignity and love on the day.

If you are the only one giving the eulogy you must talk to all the family and friends to make sure that your view is not the only one represented. If you are one of a number of people who have been asked to speak, identify the group you are to represent and tailor the words to meet this need. You may know only one aspect of the person, whereas when you talk to others you will find their perceptions may be different. Encourage others to talk about the person and take those snippets of memories to add to your own.

There are some questions you need to answer beforehand:

- Are there any sensitive issues that you should not mention?
- How long do you need to speak?
- Who else is speaking (so that you do not go over the same ground)?
- At what stage during the ceremony will you be expected to speak?

Depending on whom you are representing, whether it is family or friends, you should paint a broad-brush picture of the person, pertinent to that group. Try to encapsulate the person's character, humour, pursuits and habits, as well as expressing how and why they were loved.

Your style of eulogy must respect the character of the person. Think how they would like to be remembered. If they lived their life in quiet content, your words must reflect this; if they were a party animal, then find some humour to match this. Sometimes deciding on a theme 'characteristic' can help you to structure the speech.

Approach this speech in the same way as any other. Preparation is the key message. By its nature this speech will be full of personal material, but it should not come across as simply a string of memories. Strengthen what you say with examples of how this person's life touched others. Visualising the occasion will be of enormous help in delivering this speech successfully.

This is one speech that I recommend you write out in full. If you prefer to use speech notes on the day do so, but take a well-typed copy of the speech with you just in case you are overcome with emotion and need someone else to read it for you. Your documented speech should also be given to the family as a memento.

If you find your emotions swell at various points while you are speaking, take your time, breathe deeply and give yourself that reassuring signal until you can pull yourself together again. Remember, it is a most special privilege to be able to vocalise the depth and breadth of feeling that the audience has for such a loved one.

In researching and preparing this challenging speech, consider some of the following points:

- What were the key highlights of the person's life?
  - family, social, career, community, sport, interests
- What were their characteristics?
  - touch on their beliefs, philosophies and integrity
  - their faith
  - their love of family and friends
  - their work ethic
  - their humour
  - their foibles

- Personalise your words
  - for the family
  - for the friends
  - for yourself
- Did they have any favourite poetry, book, song that you can quote?

Speak to the funeral directors or minister to get an idea of when you need to speak. Sit towards the front of the church or venue so that you will be able to move to the lectern easily.

On the day, if you are concerned about your reaction when you reach the lectern, ask your partner, a relative or a friend to join you there. Organise someone beforehand to take over to read your speech if you are unable to continue.

If the person has lived a full and long life, your choice of words should express that this is a celebration of a life well lived and the gratitude that you feel to have known them and shared part of their journey.

A eulogy for a young life 'cut short' is always extremely painful but the same guidelines, where relevant, should be used to develop the speech.

Write from your heart and from family and friends' hearts. Deliver your words with courage and you will know you have succeeded.

Any quotes that you use will be pertinent to the person but I include a beautiful quote from Dr Kubler-Ross, that I hope will bring comfort to you as you undertake this difficult speech.

We are not powerless specks of dust drifting around in the wind, blown by random destiny. We are, each of us, like beautiful snowflakes – unique, and born for a specific reason and purpose.

ELISABETH KUBLER-ROSS

WORKSHOP
PRESENTATIONS

I hear and I forget. I see and I remember. I do and I understand.

If you have not presented a workshop before, here is the basic knowledge you need. You will need to develop a range of techniques that stimulate adult learning. You must recognise the importance of building a rapport with your audience, and use a variety of other strategies, including timing, to implement and enhance your message. Last but not least, the choice of venue is crucial to comfortable learning.

A workshop is a short course for a small group which focuses upon problem-solving and/or gaining knowledge of a particular subject. If you are considering presenting a workshop, I believe you should have some mileage in public speaking. Presenting a workshop is complex and demanding and you need to have a stockpile of experience in public speaking and audience interaction to draw from. This will enable you to cope with and manage the processes involved in this exacting presentation. If you are a new speaker and it is your goal to present workshops for your work or interest, I suggest that you undertake a 'train the trainer' course with TAFE or some other qualified learning centre. Most industry skill-based workshops require qualifications and, once you have achieved this basic certification, it opens your options in this teaching area.

There are many workshop presenters around who have no formal training. Their knowledge and expertise have probably been gained from experience and their own studies. Each time they have presented a workshop they have gained more knowledge of how, where and what to do and, more importantly, what *not* to do.

The opportunity to present a workshop may arise because you have specialist knowledge or people have seen you speak with authority on a subject and this has sparked their interest and they want to learn more.

Other presenters see an opening in the market to present a workshop that has commercial appeal. Evening colleges, community centres and conference or event management companies are useful targets when trying to sell a workshop. The most popular workshops follow society's current trends, as reflected in the magazines we read and the television we watch. Quality workshops concerned with self-development, spiritual philosophies and lifestyle or craft skills are all well received in today's market.

While some speakers have substantial knowledge of a subject, it does not necessarily follow that they will be able to transfer this learning effectively to a wider audience. A work-shop presenter needs to have, or develop, other characteristics or skills to be successful. You are ahead of the game if you are naturally caring, respectful of others' experience, flexible, are prepared to shelve your own ego, and are sincere in your encouragement of others. A good workshop presenter is more facilitator than teacher. These attributes, whether natural or learned, are vital if your students are going to enjoy the process and come away retaining knowledge that they can effectively use in their lives.

Adult learning

Recently a friend of mine attended a one-day workshop. She had been eagerly looking forward to the prospect of learning more about a subject that was close to her heart. She was ready to participate in the learning process and firmly anticipated that by the end of the day she would acquire new skills and knowledge that she could use to her benefit.

> *A good workshop presenter is more facilitator than teacher.*

Later, when I asked her about the workshop, she reported that it had been a disappointment. While she did get some excellent resource notes that she thought would be useful, she did not really did not gain significantly from the time or dollars spent. While the presenter certainly knew his subject, he did not appear to understand the audience's expectations and limitations. He lectured solidly, illuminating key facts with a magnificent high-tech PowerPoint presentation. This was great for the first hour but when this became the focus for most of the day, give or take the odd break, it was information overload for the audience.

The presenter did not encourage questions and was uncomfortable with anyone who interrupted his flow of rhetoric. When he asked questions, they were quite complicated, and people had difficulty in answering. My friend thought this made them feel inadequate, as it certainly undermined her confidence. She observed that the majority of the audience reaction was the same as hers and this was a day to be endured in order to get the knowledge that they wanted. She said her 'feelings fluctuated between boredom and anger'. Presented in a different medium, such as a lecture hall, and using smaller chunks of time, this presenter's information would probably have been well received.

I am sure that this workshop was given with the very best intentions of increasing people's knowledge. Unfortunately the presenter did not make an effort to understand the audience's needs and their limitations, or even grasp the importance of developing a warm relationship with them. Had he attended to these important issues he would have been able to create an encouraging environment to support the learning process.

To produce a successful workshop, not only must you have excellent knowledge of and resource material related to your subject, but you must understand that the following elements are vital in the process of adult learning:

- Begin with the premise that we all learn in different ways.
- Develop plans and strategies to help adults learn.
- Facilitate rather than teach.
- Develop a rapport with the audience.
- Respect others' life experiences.
- Put your ego on hold.
- Be resourceful and flexible.
- Adopt a caring, nurturing approach.
- Learn how to give sincere, positive reinforcement.

Key features of adult learning

- Teaching adults generates different challenges from those faced when teaching children. Each of us is unique and we learn in different ways. Some people are more analytical and prefer to learn in a step-by-step fashion (a left-brain function). Others prefer to learn by looking first at the bigger picture, then going on to specifics (a right-brain function).

- Importantly, as adults, we need to feel free to direct our own learning processes.
- As adults we have a lot at risk when we try new behaviours or attempt new skills. We put our egos on the line and our self-esteem takes a pasting if we do not get it right the first time, especially when we are doing it in front of other people.
- Adults do not like long lectures or periods of inactivity.
- New information or ideas that conflict with our beliefs take us longer to absorb.
- Adults are goal-orientated. We are practical beings, so any information or workshop activities need to be relevant to our specific needs in order for us to integrate that information easily and retain it.
- Like children, we gain considerably from positive reinforcement.
- The physical learning environment is important to adults. To learn effectively we need to feel comfortable and relaxed. The time of day will also have an effect on our ability to take in information. First thing in the morning some people may be only half-awake and by mid-afternoon we are tiring and our ability to retain information decreases.
- Many people attend workshops because they want to gain specific knowledge or a specific skill that they need for either work or a particular interest. Increasing their sense of self-esteem and pleasure is also a motivating factor in the learning experience. People who are going through life-changing events are also likely to seek out workshops or other courses as a coping strategy, as they weather these changes in their lives.

Planning a workshop to enhance adult learning

I am always ready to learn although I do not always like to be taught.

WINSTON CHURCHILL

To give a successful workshop you need to take into account all the factors that are involved in adult learning. Thus, a workshop has to have plenty of stimuli to accommodate the fact that we all learn in different ways and to take into account that adults hate long periods of inactivity. The presenter must value and encourage each member of the group. They must be sensitive to the fact that participants may be nervous or frightened about embarrassing themselves. The presenter must understand that, above all things, we want to retain our dignity. At the same time, most people who go to workshops want to learn and are goal-oriented.

So how do we design the workshop to meet most people's needs? The answer is through planning. You will need to mind map (or use your preferred method of planning) the overall concept and then mind map specific issues that arise from this. You will need to consider some or all of the planning issues listed below.

- Identify your primary objective (what you want your students to gain from the workshop).

- Identify secondary and/or other objectives.
- Develop strategies to meet these objectives, including the use of a variety of techniques to stimulate and reinforce learning capacity.
- Plan ways to develop a rapport with your audience.
- Develop a process to evaluate outcomes.
- Plan the timing of the workshop.
- Investigate suitable venues, or if the venue has been decided for you, investigate the most effective way to use the room and staging to suit your purpose.

Now let's look more closely at some of these issues.

Use a variety of techniques to stimulate and reinforce learning capacity

Because a workshop is a short course, the teaching approach used must necessarily be different to that of traditional educational practices that are employed for long-term learning experiences. The key to success in learning in short bites is to make learning fun and accessible or, as the educational experts like to call it, 'serious play'. Group interaction is vital and strategies should be developed to provide participants with opportunities for working in teams, appointing their own leaders to report back to the group, and group discussion.

Useful tools in achieving this group interaction are:

- **Video clips, tape recordings**
  These should be clips, no longer than five to seven minutes.
- **Problem-solving games, quizzes, or questionnaires**
  Divide the group into teams and allow them to compete for fun awards.
- **Hands-on activities**
  First show participants how and then encourage them to try techniques or activities themselves.
- **Group discussion**
  Empower students to voice their thoughts and experiences.

This is learning from others' experiences. Remember to encourage the quieter students.

- **Brainstorming**

  Use small groups or the class as a whole to brainstorm possible solutions to problems. Record all thoughts on a flip chart so that these can be collated and qualified.

- **Role-plays**

  Always be very sensitive to people's feelings. For some, role-plays might be their worst nightmare so, if you recognise this fear in them, do not push them into doing something they would hate. Unless of course the workshop is about 'over-coming your fears'!

For these techniques you might use a range of audiovisual equipment – a whiteboard and markers, flipcharts and markers, an overhead projector, video facilities and screen, CD or tape-recording facilities.

Develop a rapport with your audience

- When people register, give them a large, easily read name badge to wear. On the tables have tent cards in front of each participant with their name printed on it.
- Make sure you use people's name each time you speak to them.
- Find time before the workshop starts to introduce yourself and have a few words with them.
- Use humour and storytelling to make people feel at ease and increase their enjoyment throughout the workshop.
- Do not make questions too hard or too easy. If questions are too easy you risk looking patronising. If they are too hard you may embarrass people if they cannot answer. Ideally the right balance is somewhere in between. You know you have succeeded when they can answer and it is obvious they feel good about it. Plan the style of questions carefully.

- When you ask a question, make sure it is about material that you have already covered. It is a turn-off when you ask a question that you think people should know about your subject but have not given them any reference.
- Plan a variety of positive, reinforcing statements and vocabulary so that what you say sounds fresh rather than trite.
- Be sensitive to clues, verbal or physical, of people's discomfort or anxiety.
- After you have introduced yourself, ask participants to introduce themselves and indicate what they want to achieve from attending your workshop. You can then go on to weave some of these responses into the overview of what students can expect to gain from this learning experience.
- Be observant of people's learning needs and, where possible, if you feel someone may be confused, try to rephrase your words or use another technique to get the point across.
- The more you involve your audience in a responsible and caring way, the more they will enjoy it and be able to retain the knowledge.
- Deliver what you promise and run to time.

Develop a process to evaluate outcomes

You will need to develop a method for evaluating how much the student has learned from the time spent with you. The content and potential outcomes of the course will drive the format. A simple evaluation process that works well is to ask students to evaluate the relevance of the workshop to their needs, as they defined them at the beginning of the class.

This evaluation of the course will prove invaluable when you are planning your next workshop.

Plan the timing of the workshop

The time of day affects our responses and retention abilities. Plan your agenda around peak learning times to maximise people's learning.

Early morning is not the best time as some people may not be fully awake. The majority of your audience will have had many domestic issues to deal with before leaving home and certainly most will have had to battle with the early-morning traffic or commuter transport. This is the time to allow people to get acquainted with each other and to talk about their aspirations for the workshop. This is the time for you to preview the course objectives and give students an overview of what they can expect from the day.

As the morning progresses, responses will increase. By mid-morning they are peaking and this is the best time to incorporate heavy-duty information or activities. The lunchtime break slows progress down. Get straight back into things after the break because by mid-afternoon people are tired and their responses are low.

Make the best use of the venue and environment

- If the choice of venue is within your control make sure that it is, as they say in real estate, 'well appointed'. A well-maintained and stylish venue will create the right springboard for people's physical and psychological comfort.
- The room should be big enough for the group to move around and complete different activities that may be required.
- The room should be well ventilated or air-conditioned. The air-conditioning should just be a little on the cool side to keep everyone awake.

- The furniture should be set up 'classroom style' (chairs and tables). The seating should be comfortable. Tables should have notepads, pencils and an eraser for each participant. Jugs of water that are refreshed during the course of the workshop and breath mints are also necessary.
- Lighting is important. The room should be well lit or make use of natural light from windows. If there is a fantastic view from a window, do be careful – people looking at views can easily go off into a land far, far away from the activities of the moment.
- Test all the audiovisual equipment.
- Preferably choose a venue where the food and drink is known to be good and presented well. It will make your students feel pampered.
- Have upbeat music playing at the beginning of each fresh start – first thing in the morning, after the morning coffee break, after lunch and after the afternoon tea break. The music will increase the excitement and generate the necessary tension to give an edge. The volume should be a little louder than normal but not so loud that people cannot hear each other speak.
- If it is a full-day workshop, consider the catering arrangements. Alternate muffins and cookies with fruit for breaks. Lunch should be light. Avoid serving alcohol if you want people to focus effectively. If catering is not available, consider how you are going to organise coffee breaks and meal times. Asking people to bring their own sandwich for lunch is fine, but tea and coffee should be supplied.

WORKSHOP MOTIVATIONAL QUOTATIONS

Vertical thinking is digging the same hole deeper.
Lateral thinking is trying again elsewhere.

EDWARD DE BONO, *Six Thinking Hats*

The only dumb question is a question you don't ask.

PAUL MACCREADY

If you think you can or think you can't, you're right.

HENRY FORD

Everybody is ignorant, only on different subjects.

WILL ROGERS

Your brain is like a sleeping giant.

TONY BUZAN

Plutarch, the ancient Greek philosopher, summed up the perfect training for a workshop when he said: 'The mind is not a vessel to be filled, but a fire to be ignited'. Just get the other elements of building a rapport, providing comfortable environment and appropriate timing right, and you will have a runaway success.

DEBATES

It is better to debate a question without settling it,
than to settle a question without debating it.

JOSEPH JOUBERT, *French philosopher, 1754–1824*

What is a debate and what skills do you need to take part in one? See how
to build the case for either the Affirmative or Negative and specifics on the
different speakers' responsibilities.

Debating is believed to have started in Ancient Greece where debate of political issues was part of their democracy. In Athens citizens met to debate what the laws should be. People were taught the art of debating and learned to argue on both sides of an issue in order to understand it more fully.

The Oxford Union Society is recognised as one of the world's foremost debating societies. Known simply as the Oxford Union, it is a private debating society, not to be confused with the Oxford University Student Union which is the student body of the university. The Oxford Union was founded in 1823 and draws its membership mainly from the University of Oxford. It is a unique institution where some of the world's greatest leaders have voiced their political beliefs and philosophies. In 1933, six years before the outbreak of World War II, an Oxford Union debate caused a huge controversy when it passed the motion that 'This House will in no circumstances fight for its King and Country'. Winston Churchill branded it 'that abject, squalid, shameless avowal'.

In 1960 we saw the first televised head-to-head debates between American presidential candidates. The compelling John Kennedy and the hardworking but less appealing Richard Nixon thrashed it out in front of millions of viewers. Kennedy outperformed Nixon and the age of TV politics had arrived.

Here in Australia the art of the debate is fashionable not only in our universities, but also in our schools. In New South Wales, the Department of Education runs the Primary Schools Debating Championships, open to students in Year 6 and below. I was honoured to be a guest adjudicator for a couple of years and was completely won over by these dynamic young students who articulated their clever logic with such stage presence.

The Australian Debating Federation, an organisation which is continually active in organising the National Schools Debating Competition, determined to take on the wider task of making it a global competition. In 1988 the World Schools Debating Championships were started and Australia hosted the first championships in Sydney. In recent years comedy debates have also become compulsive television viewing.

This chapter targets the novice debater. The information provided is purposely simple and is designed to give you an overview of what to expect if you are invited to debate. Because it would need a book rather than a chapter to cover the intricacies of debating, this chapter does not touch on the knottier issues of debating such as 'truisms', 'circular defini-tions' or 'squirrelling'. If you need more in-depth information I suggest you investigate attending a debating workshop in your state. These are normally run by local universities or by a debating society.

If you are invited to be a panel member in a debate you will need to investigate the style and format of the debate with the organiser. While debates must follow specific rules, there are slight differences in debating styles and formats around the world and even in individual debating societies. Differences may include the number of speakers, opportunities for input from the floor, timing and speaking order but importantly the rules of conflict are basically the same. The information given here is based upon a more commonly used Australian debating style. Later in the chapter you will find Lyndey Milan, Celebrity Tipper, refers to Oxford rules which are in line with the rules shown here. In the popular comedy debates that are staged frequently on television and at live events, the 'rules' are broken frequently as these occasions are less about the rules of debate and more about the comedy of the performance.

What is a debate?

A debate consists of two teams of three, whose object is to prove that the other team has the flawed argument. A proposition, or put more simply, a topic for debate is given to the teams. One team will justify the Affirmative case and the other argues for the Negative case. They can also be referred to as the Proposition and Opposition.

What skills do I need to debate?

Many people shy away from debating as it does require taking a risk. You cannot necessarily guarantee the subject you are going to get. You cannot guarantee whether you will speak on the Affirmative or Negative team. Without previous experience it can be a scary ride. I love to watch a debate and am in awe of the skill and quick wits of the speakers. Although I, personally, am a lousy debater that does not mean that I couldn't improve my skills if challenged. I think it is like doing a crossword, difficult the first few times until you are in the swing of it. Then it becomes easier and, from my observations, definitely enjoyable.

There are a number of good reasons to embrace the skill of debating. It teaches you to think more critically about political and social issues. It trains you to look at an argument from different perspectives, to question your assumptions and long-held beliefs. It forces you to research your information and encourages the development of logical reasoning.

In a debate you will use all the skills that you have learned in creating and presenting a speech. A debate is a verbal stoush and as a speaker you have to convey this with your posture, attitude, voice and body language. You cannot take the quieter, measured approach in debating; it demands energy and vitality. Your presentation should be more a performance that makes use of grander gestures and a stronger voice.

Your argument must be centred on the pros and cons of both cases; never resort to personal remarks about the other team.

Building a case

Prior to the debate itself you will probably meet with your fellow team members to develop your team's case. The case (argument) is built from interpreting the definition or topic statement (often referred to as the 'motion'), identifying the central premise of the unified message that your team wants to convey and deciding on the different factors of material that can be used to support your claims and which team members will present these.

Defining the case

The definition of a case is vital for both teams. I find the best advice on defining the case comes from the New South Wales Department of Education and Training handbook and guide to debating, *Taking the Initiative*, which recommends that teams should first 'Isolate the issue of the debate. Decide what issue is at the centre of the proposition before even thinking about the definition of the subject'. Defining this issue at the centre of the debate restricts the boundaries of the debate so that the discussion focuses on a specific area. Often a debate can be won or lost on the interpretation of the definition of the motion.

A team's interpretation of the proposition must be able to be justified clearly. Each speaker must parallel the interpretation of the definition as they present the different elements of the debate.

Definition of the case should not rely or stand on a definition taken from the dictionary. Claiming that the definition is right because it comes from the dictionary is not acceptable. While the teams should look closely at key words and phrases and see how they affect the proposition, it is important that they define the motion as a whole.

Most importantly, the definition should be reasonable.

The Affirmative team must be careful not to give too broad a definition, as it may provide the opportunity for the Negative team to take the initiative, but equally a definition that is too narrow may leave the team with limited opportunities to argue.

The Negative team's preparation must always take into account that their case is valid only in relation to the case put by the Affirmative. Nevertheless they must plan their argument in case the definition can or must be challenged. The team must try to consider all possible definitions that the Affirmative may choose so that they are prepared as best as they are able. The Negative may take one of these approaches:

- **Straight negation** – not generally advised as it exerts no extra pressure on the Affirmative
- **Not generally true** – allows the Negative to seem reasonable and throws the burden of proof back on the Affirmative
- **Proving the converse** – a reversal of the stated proposition, for example 'that girls are brighter than boys' becomes an attempt to prove 'that boys are brighter than girls'.

Central premise of the argument

Both teams should decide on the central premise, theme or core statement of their arguments. The central premise is best understood as the direction or stance of the team's argument. It will be able to be clearly identified and developed as the team defines their approach to the argument. It should be able to be expressed in either a single sentence or, if necessary, several short statements. This central premise (which as you have read is central to any successful speech) will ensure that all speakers are consistent in speaking to the case.

Speaking responsibilities

Be guided by the more experienced members of your team who will decide the speaking positions depending on the experience and skills of each speaker. The team will then decide on how the various tasks or lines of argument are to be allocated. A popular way to split these tasks is to break them down into elements. These elements may cover things like culture, politics, society, logistics, and so on. These elements can then be distributed to the speakers.

FIRST AFFIRMATIVE

As the first speaker of the Affirmative you are in a unique position, as you do not have to respond to any other speaker. Your role is to define the subject and justify your case. You will need to outline the Affirmative team argument and indicate who will present the different elements of your case. Normally this role is given to the least experienced member, as they will be able to script their contribution without the anxiety of rebutting opposition arguments.

FIRST NEGATIVE

As first speaker of the Negative you will need to evaluate the Affirmative definition, either accepting or rejecting it. If you reject it, you will need to justify this and present the Negative team's definition.

You must outline the Negative argument and indicate who will present the different elements of your case. The first Negative speaker needs to have more experience for this role. Your team will be absorbing the Affirmative argument and will give you written directions or support before you even stand up to speak.

SECOND AFFIRMATIVE

As second speaker for the Affirmative, if the definition is still an issue, you must clarify this. You will need to rebut the Negative first speaker's case and argue the issues arising from it. You will need to present your allocated elements of the Affirmative case. Normally the second speaker is the one who presents the most important arguments of the case.

SECOND NEGATIVE

As second speaker for the Negative, if definition is still an issue you will also need to clarify this. You will need to rebut the Affirmative's case to date and argue the issues arising. You need to present your own allocated material. Again, as second speaker, you will probably shoulder the weightier parts of the argument.

Both second speakers should be careful not to spend too much time on refutation as they will not have sufficient time to present their case. Allow approximately half the allocated speaking time for developing your team's case.

THIRD AFFIRMATIVE

As third speaker for the Affirmative your role is to present the Affirmative case in the most effective way. Compare and contrast both cases, highlighting again the weaknesses in the Negative arguments and the strengths of the Affirmative case. Generally most rules discourages the third speaker from presenting new material. Normally the role of third speaker is given to the most experienced member.

THIRD NEGATIVE

As third speaker for the Negative your position is to present the Negative case in the best light. You will need to compare and contrast both cases, underscoring the weaknesses in the Affirmative arguments and the strengths in the Negative case. Again, most rules generally do not allow the third speaker to present any new material. This role is given to the most experienced member of the team.

Timing

Timing can vary, so you will need to check this with the organisers. Normally, a bell or some other signal is given a minute before you should finish speaking. If you exceed the time another signal will be given.

Adjudication of the debate

Experienced and qualified adjudicators evaluate formal debates and decide on the winning team. Generally they give both teams a good understanding of how and why they reached their conclusion. In most comedy or fun debates the adjudicator will provide some guidance as to the effectiveness of both arguments but will call on the audience to judge the final outcome.

Formal debates are judged on three elements: matter, manner and method. 'Matter' refers to everything that is said in the debate, that is, the content of the argument. 'Manner' refers to the way speakers present – your debating stance, eye contact with your audience, the fluency of your argument and platform presence. 'Method' deals with the way you and your team have organised the material and the form in which your have structured your overall argument.

CELEBRITY TIP

Is your debate serious or for entertainment? Most of my experience since leaving school is with the latter style. In this case, view the debate as a piece of theatre. You are there to convince the audience (and the adjudicator) that the way you present your argument is the most convincing, no matter how ridiculous the topic. So go for it – but first make sure whether or not you are being judged on the Oxford rules!

Make sure you state your team's premise and the team line, rebut whatever the other team may have said before you, and then let loose. Remember, you only get one opportunity to make a first impression, so make it count. So open *and* close strongly. You may choose to use simple props to great effect (quite outside the rules!). Use humour but never be nasty – and remember, laughing at yourself can be an effective means to get the audience on side. The very best 'spontaneous' debates still have all the hallmarks of any good speech – forward thought, planning, cooperation with other speakers, knowledge of the topic and a good dose of personality.

LYNDEY MILAN

If you have read this chapter in close detail, it must be because you have a keen interest in debating. The primary benefit of taking part in a debate is that you will learn new skills that will help you face any speaking assignment. When you first consider being part of a debate the rules can seem overwhelming but think of it this way: if tiny tots can ski and debate so well, then adults can certainly can afford to 'give it a go'.

FORMAL
SPEECHES

Nothing is so unbelievable that oratory cannot make it acceptable.

CICERO, *Roman orator, 46 BC*

Learn what you need to know if you are invited to speak at a seminar, conference, masterclass, an awards or presentation ceremony, or to make a testimonial speech. The chapter concludes with a section on how to make a gracious 'off-the-cuff' acceptance speech.

Much of the information presented in the early part of this chapter relates to 'platform'-style speaking assignments, the sort of formal speeches that are required at conferences, seminars or masterclasses. Later in the chapter we look at some specific speaking assignments that call for a slightly different focus – the testimony speech and the acceptance speech.

A seminar is devoted to presentations on a particular subject and differs from a conference in that it is a shorter version, normally only a day or even less. While being longer in duration, a conference usually covers a broader range of topics which target a specific market. A masterclass is a class that is given by a recognised and respected expert in a specific field.

General guidelines for conference-style speeches

Unless you are a very experienced presenter, speaking at a conference will 'raise the bar' of your stress levels. The organising body has obviously chosen you for your knowledge and expertise. As well as sharing your interest or vocation in the subject matter, the audience will be made up of people who have paid money to attend. You will be very aware that their expectations are high. The best way to reduce and control your stress is through preparation, preparation and more preparation.

No matter whether you are a pilot going through all the standard checks before take-off or an event organiser ticking off items on a to-do list, all safe and effective planning starts with a checklist. Below is a list of standard procedures to follow in preparing your speech.

Preparation checklist

- Send a written reply to confirm your acceptance and the arrangements made.
- Diarise the date of speaking and the deadline for speakers' papers, audiovisual requirements and biographical details. Work out how long you will have to prepare in order to meet the deadline comfortably.
- Ask for a written brief from the organiser (if this was not provided with the invitation). What do they want you to cover specifically in your presentation?
- Organise a meeting with the organiser (if necessary).

   If the brief does not quite fit with your particular expertise, or if you feel the presentation needs to come from a slightly different level or angle, you will need to discuss this with the organiser. Both parties need to be confident that they are meeting the desired outcomes for the delegates.

- Research the audience. The organiser should be able to give you a general idea of the anticipated audience numbers and demographics.
- Plan your preparation with timelines to achieve the different aspects of the presentation.
- Include any necessary research. Don't procrastinate or fool yourself that there is plenty of time.
- Decide on your method of presentation. What audiovisual requirements do you need?
- Prepare your speech. Make sure your speech reflects the agreed brief.
- Time your speech. Speaking to time is essential at a conference. When rehearsing the speech privately, ensure that the timing is always slightly under for a lengthy presentation. Aim for two to three minutes under time, as you can be sure that on the day, with audience interaction, it will run longer.
- Type the speech out in full, according to the organiser's instructions. Often the organiser will give specific directions about the font and spacing to be used. Send your paper to the organiser in plenty of time.
- Prepare the audiovisual presentation.

It is very tempting to use a high-tech presentation with images that can slide, starburst, flip and fade, but take care that it is not too distracting. A full-blown razzamatazz electronic presentation should not upstage you, the speaker.

If you prefer to use an overhead projector, consider whether it is in your best interests to control the projector yourself or brief someone else to change the transparencies for you. If the latter, you must give them a script or a signal when you are ready to move onto the next transparency.

- Rehearse, rehearse and rehearse.

  Rehearse everything – the speech and the media presentation – until you feel very confident.

- Recheck the demographics of the audience. These may have changed a little and you do need to take this into account. If it is vital for you to change anything in your presentation, check with the organiser to see if you can make changes to your paper. If not, you will need to tell the audience that changes have been made and they should note this.

- Check with the organiser that everything is on track.
  Find out about parking.

- Arrive early at the venue.

  The organiser will normally give you an indication of how early you should be but always arrive at least an hour earlier than you need to. This enables you to gauge the mood of the conference, meet the emcee, meet the audiovisual technician and the organiser, and check that all is well. It also gives you time to get a cup of tea. Find the bathroom and, while there, do a few deep-breathing exercises.

  Most importantly, arriving early reduces the stresses attached to running late. If you are travelling interstate, arrive the evening before and stay overnight, if possible, so that you do not run the risk of the plane being cancelled or rerouted.

The brief

The effectiveness of the speaker's brief plays a major part in the overall success of this style of speaking assignment. The style and content of the program is directed by the conference objectives. The major objective of any conference is to achieve an organic and dynamic program that will attract delegates and meet the needs of their organisation.

Organisers look for speakers with a depth of knowledge in their particular field, who have the ability to deliver each of the selected elements of the program. Therefore you need to read and digest the brief thoroughly. If you have any concerns or different thoughts about the direction of the brief, you must discuss them to the organiser. They might be able to satisfy your concerns and accommodate any changes, if this does not compromise the integrity of what they are trying to achieve.

Speakers who do not understand the value of sticking to the brief put themselves at risk of being seen as less credible.

CELEBRITY TIP

Probably the most important piece of information you need to get to enable you to make a totally professional presentation is a proper brief. In this document, you will be given all the pertinent information that you need to do the job at hand.

No matter what type of presentation you are doing, you always need to know what time you start and finish – where it is you are to present and with what type of audiovisual assistance.

Also it is imperative that you know what the message or main objective of your presentation is and to whom this message is being disseminated.

It all comes back to knowing why you are there and how to fulfil that responsibility, knowing where and when you are to work and knowing what the main message is for you to impart.

Apart from all that, remember the 'performance-factor' – always smile and be personable. The age of the 'superstar' was in the 1980s – we are in the new age now, where you are appreciated for what information and expertise you can provide.

PETER HOWARD

Timing

Generally, allocated time of speeches at conferences is generous and can range from twenty to thirty minutes. Keynote speakers are given longer. You will have a lot to say and once you start pulling it all together you will find that you can fill the allotted time very easily and could probably go on for longer. It is always seductive having a generous portion of time to speak on a subject close to your heart. However, be very careful as time waits for no speaker. When you rehearse, note the timing of key places in your notes so that you know easily and clearly how close you are to time.

Presentation

Audiences do not like sitting for long periods without activity so their response and retention of what you have to say will depend on how you create your presentation. It is a good idea to break your presentation into three easy bites, using a different treatment or style for each of these short periods so that your speech continually refreshes and intrigues the listener. The first part of your speech may be more formal as you introduce and outline your presentation; the second part may be all whistles and bells; and then the third part might move into a more reflective style.

You can achieve variety with different styles by way of a PowerPoint presentation if that is your preferred method of presenting, or simply by using different electronic media to create the effect you want.

If you are using a PowerPoint presentation make sure you do not simply read the key headings without fleshing out these points. Remember to keep your body facing the audience when presenting any audiovisual equipment – use the laptop screen to follow your presentation.

Managing the tasks and time

Always consider how you are going to manage all the tasks you have set yourself. These tasks may simply be speaking and watching the clock, or they be more involved, such as giving an electronic presentation, as well as speaking and watching the clock.

You must be comfortable with what you do and you must be capable of doing it well and fluently. It is a question of knowing your strengths and weaknesses. It is fine if you have always been able to pat your head while rubbing your stomach (or is it the other way round?). But if you are a 'do one job at a time'-type person, who perhaps does not have a great deal of speaking experience, you should find the way that will present the fewest difficulties when it comes to presenting, especially when it comes to using electronic media.

Good strategies for single-minded people are to make sure you are at the venue early so that you can do a rehearsal, with the audiovisual technician doing a bit of hand-holding until you feel confident with the remote control. The technician will be very happy to do this because they too have a vested interest in making sure that everything runs smoothly.

Either the organiser or emcee can be persuaded into the role of surrogate timer for you. You still need to keep your watch on the lectern but ask the emcee or organiser to give you some agreed time signals, whether by a bell, or one of them standing up (obviously the person must be in your line of sight).

The organiser

Always make friends with the organiser. They appreciate courtesy and civility, as often the speakers they deal with are high maintenance. Speakers who respect the rules of the game, that is, lodge speaker's papers, biographical details and audiovisual requirements on time, are going to be appreciated.

All event organisers I know, and I include myself in this, want to please people. They love to help and see everything go super well. They will certainly help to make your path smoother.

CELEBRITY TIP

During your career, you may present in many different locations and to many different audiences. It is important for you to know where you fit in the program. If you are the keynote speaker, make sure you set the mood for the rest of the seminar or conference – this is your responsibility. Always start and finish on time, as there are others to follow and a schedule to maintain. You may be a member of a panel. Greediness is not appreciated anywhere anymore, so make sure you stick to your information and don't poach other speakers' material.

PETER HOWARD

Using plain English

Remember the rules of speech: use language that you are comfortable with and that you are confident your audience will understand. Avoid gratuitous use of jargon, even in an industry-based conference.

Don't make your presentation too heavy, even if it is an intense subject; find some way to lighten the presentation either with humour, anecdotal material or storytelling. Remember, you need to put different textures, light and shade into the presentation to keep the audience's attention.

Question time

If your session is billed to incorporate a question and answer time you must plan for this. Question time can be tricky, both for inexperienced and experienced speakers. To confidently face question time you need to consider the following:

- Check and double-check your facts and the sources that you refer to in your speech. If there is anything ambiguous in the speech, clarify it or remove it.
- Unless questioners use a microphone, always repeat the question so that the broader audience can hear it.
- If the question is longwinded, paraphrase it to the person and check that this is what they asked.
- Answer the question as briefly as you can. Don't go off on a tangent as one thought leads to another. Be very disciplined in managing questions as it can be disappointing for the audience if the opportunity for questions is lessened by answers that are too lengthy.
- If you do not know the answer to the question, don't waffle as you try to regain ground. Admit that you do not know the answer. Suggest the person sees you after the presentation and you will take their details and if possible get back to them with an answer.
- If the questioner is antagonistic, be courteous but firm. If someone is looking for a confrontation you need to nip it in the bud as quickly as possible. Don't try to justify your position; simply, and pleasantly, agree to differ.
- Be aware of time, as it will literally take wings during question time. Ask the emcee to manage question time for you by identifying speakers and watching the clock.

After the conference

Most conferences ask delegates to fill in an exit survey. When collated this provides an accurate picture of the audience's opinions of the speakers and conference management. This type of information is invaluable for you. I am sure there will be a considerable amount of warm and fuzzies that will give your ego a lift but you will learn more from the critique.

Send a letter of thanks to the organiser and ask if it is possible for you to receive feedback on your presentation. Providing the organiser does not have any conflict with this, I am sure they will be happy to do it for you.

Panel speaker

Panel discussions are a great vehicle to put some texture into conference programming. They are popular with audiences, as a group of respected panellists is able to give them valuable information, as well as bring contrasting views on the subject.

The panel is led by a chairperson or emcee who introduces the subject and members of the panel. The object of most panel discussions is to stimulate thinking and provide delegates with cutting-edge information. However, some organisers may wish to achieve set outcomes from the project.

If you have never been a panel member before, these are the types of questions you need to ask when agreeing to take part:

- Who are your fellow panel members?
- Who is the chairperson or emcee?
- What are the fellow presenters' qualifications?
- What objectives do the organisers have for these discussions?
- How much time will be allocated for you to present your views before 'open' discussion time?
- Will the Chair take questions from the audience?

When you have all these answers, start planning your presentation. While more time is allocated to this program session, you will still need to be reasonably brief in your presentation. Condense your presentation to key factors that will meet the objectives for the discussion.

Do your homework and find out the other speakers' viewpoints. Use this information to plan your position in the overall scheme of the discussion. Think ahead of possible questions that could arise from this convergence of different thinking and values.

You can understand that timing will be pivotal in this assignment. The chairperson will be looking at this critically. Timing must be correct or you will be cut short. Put your watch where you can see it clearly. A tip that is known to work very well for speakers who find timing their presentation a bit tricky is to mark the face of your watch with a red pen, just a dot, to indicate when your time is up.

Of course, this is a great learning experience for you too as you are going to be stimulated and challenged by the ideas of others. If the conference is being recorded get a copy of the tape for your reference and own mental debriefing.

Send a letter of thanks to the chairperson, organiser and other panel members – always a good PR exercise. Ask the organiser to keep you in the loop with any feedback received.

Testimony or 'tell your story' speech

For the purposes of this book, I will define 'testimony' as a presentation by a role model who is a shining example to the audience of the benefits or achievements of a product, service or a learned behaviour. In most arenas, this means standing up in front of your peers and telling your story. Testimonies may include a rags-to-riches story, a journey of spiritual growth, or even how a particular product, service, or behaviour changed your life for the better.

Some of the great exponents of this style of speaking are the modern-day motivational leaders like Anthony Robbins whose followers are happy to walk across hot coals to spend time with him. As these styles of speeches are normally a case of preaching to the converted, there is always that supportive groundswell in the audience, which buoys the speaker and makes the delivery of the speech even more compelling. Network marketing, retail sales and direct sales companies use testimonial speakers to great advantage to encourage and motivate fellow associates and salespeople.

The object of the testimony is to inspire and motivate. Often the testimony can be very poignant, as people tell of degrees of hardship or disadvantage in earlier years and how they have 'risen above' all the negative issues to get to where they are today. These styles of speech work very effectively as the audience relates to the story and determines: 'If they can do it, so can I'.

This may be the first time you have been invited to speak and it will be a memorable milestone in your development. If you have been achieving quietly in the background you may be unused to the spotlight and could well be feeling anxious about what you are going say, your performance and how the audience will receive it. Put your mind at ease. This is one of the easiest speeches you can ever make. You are going to be speaking about yourself. Even if we are shy, we love it when people are interested in hearing about us. We all love to talk about ourselves; sadly we don't have the opportunity too frequently.

In a testimony speech you have the best opportunity ever to experience the real connection between you and the audience as they are hanging out to hear your story. This will show in their eyes and in their body language. They want to be motivated, they want to know how you have done it, so each word you utter will be important. Your confidence will grow and the next time you present your story, it will only improve.

When putting your story together, consider the following elements:

- Follow the guidelines for writing a speech, even though this is a story.

- A mind map will prove invaluable for this type of speech.
- The introduction should allow you to quickly get into your story. For example, 'This time two years ago I was working seven days a week, doing fourteen-hour days, ...'.
- The best testimonials make use of Ying and Yang principles, that is, they use opposing highs and lows of the story to paint the picture. In other words, tell the audience the sad, bad things and then tell them the good, better, best things of today.
- The conclusion should be uplifting, leaving your audience on a high. For example, 'I now work only when I feel like it and never when the surf is up. Believe me, if I can do it, you can do it too. Won't you join me in having the time and freedom to do the things you love best?'
- To give the very best speech you can is simple: be true to yourself. Don't be tempted to be anything but absolutely true to yourself. With apologies to Winston Churchill who is credited with this famous line: 'Never, never, never give up'.

I am sure you will leave the stage feeling elated. As this is a journey that has the potential to take you to audiences you have never dreamed of, you will find feedback invaluable. Ask a couple of people from the organisation whom you respect as speakers to provide this for you.

The more you present, the better your presentation will become. You will get used to the feelings of pre-speech nerves and learn how to manage them. You will learn to sculpt your speech with the texture of voice variation and the pause. You will make that magical connection that comes from your words and, with your words, your heart.

Acceptance speech

We have all seen and heard them, the best and worst of them, lit up on our screens: 'I would like to thank my mother, my father, Auntie Flo, Uncle John, Cousin Roger, my neighbour Mr Potter ...' – the speech that drones on through a list of people no one but family and friends know.

No matter what the award or occasion, the purpose of an acceptance speech is to accept gracefully and, where necessary, to thank relevant people.

If you are a nominee or a contestant at an awards ceremony, do you arrive with a prepared speech? Unless it is a sure-fire bet that you will receive the award, you may feel you do not want to jinx your chances, so you do not prepare anything except that enormous list of people to thank. If you are the recipient of an acknowledgement and gift at a farewell or other celebration, you will have to give a speech of acceptance.

So, more often than not, acceptance speeches are given without preparation. What can you do ahead of time to help when that moment comes and you have to stand and say thank you?

Well, in both cases, you know that the odds are shortened in favour of the possibility of making a speech. In the case of an award, it is understandable that you feel a little superstitious but this may be the memory of a lifetime for you, so take the risk, start planning what you want to say. If the company has put on a special party for your retirement or farewell, you can be confident that there will indeed be speeches praising you and acknowledging your value to the company which you will have to respond to.

An acceptance speech should primarily be an opportunity to tell people what the award or acknowledgement means to you. For most of us, this moment of recognition has meant sacrifices and hard work; it has meant a steady growth in our personal development and achievements. Hopefully it has given us a sense of worth and identity. Maybe there have been key people who have contributed to your achievements.

Prepare your 'off-the-cuff' speech by:

- taking a good length of time to think about what this recognition means to you
- using this thinking time to formulate key ideas and what you want to express
- jotting down some notes or bullet-point ideas
- thanking key people only and acknowledging generally all the others who have played a part in helping you to achieve
- not overpreparing. Your speech should still have that ad lib quality
- running over the key points again in your mind, just before you arrive at the event.

CELEBRITY TIP

If you are working from notes, but essentially adlibbing, write down your key points – then add a few subheadings, one word is often enough. For example, **Sydney Opera House** a. Tourist icon, b. Cultural mecca, c. Diverse performance. This might seem like a basic ground rule, but it's surprising how many first-time speakers ignore it.

IAN ROSS

If I were to encapsulate the philosophical message of this chapter in one word it would be preparation. Forward planning is always essential for any speech, but when you present at this level of audience expectation, it is pivotal to your success that you consider every minute detail of the work to be done prior to the event, at the event and after the event. The work you do beforehand will pay dividends for your confidence when you get to the lectern.

AFTER-DINNER OR HUMOUROUS SPEECHES

*Once you get people laughing, they're listening
and you can tell them almost anything.*

HERBERT GEORGE GARDNER, *American Playwright, 1934–2003*

*Discover how to present an entertaining speech – including the popular 'roast'
type of speech.*

By its very timing and environment, an after-dinner speech
should complement the sense of wellbeing that good food, good
wine and pleasant company have created. People expect an after-
dinner speech to be witty, clever and relevant to the occasion.
Speakers who are invited to speak at such occasions have built a
reputation for being both amusing and delivering a speech well.
But there is always a first time for everything, including an after-
dinner speech. This chapter has been written for those speakers
delivering their first after-dinner or humorous speech.

CELEBRITY TIP

One of the most disarming and endearing things you can do with your audience is include a touch of humour in your presentation; it's instant bonding. Even if it's the odd playful quip … it helps you connect.

DEBORAH HUTTON

Before writing your speech, it is vital to find out the following information:

* Who are your audience?

    You need to appreciate how your audience is made up. What age bracket does the audience fit into? Do they all have a common interest?

* Why are they at this occasion?

    Is it work-related or for relaxation? What is the unifying factor that brings them together?

* What is the occasion?

    You need to understand the significance of the occasion and how you can make your speech relevant or themed to the event or organisation.

* When is the speech to be given?

    An 'after-dinner' style of speech can be after any meal. The time of day will affect the response of your audience. If you do a breakfast meeting you will find people are ready to get out there and tackle the day and will be much more ready to take in real information; you just need to pepper it with the odd bit of humour. Lunchtime speeches need to have a bit more humour because although people's responses and retention are still peaking, as lunch is a little more relaxed, they are looking for a change of pace, especially if the event is a conference where they have been absorbing hard facts for most of the morning. In the evening a speech should be lighter in content, spiced with plenty of humour.

Creating humour

You don't need to be a stand-up comic to be a roaring success as an after-dinner speaker. If you are not a natural comedian, don't think that you have to set yourself a-joke-a-minute target. The audience is warm and mellow by the time you speak and ready to laugh at the slightest implication of humour. Getting a smile, laugh, chuckle, giggle, chortle or guffaw for a funny line that you have created is one of life's great moments.

Imagine how hard it must be to be a stand-up comedian. There is the pressure of performing to a live audience and making sure each time that the next performance is equally funny, if not more so. Imagine confronting the variety of audiences, some receptive and ready to rock on, and others indifferent to the jokes. But stand-up comics obviously love their work and their ultimate reward must be the approbation they receive from their listeners.

Edward De Bono, considered a leading authority in creative thinking, believes that humour is a typical example of lateral thinking – it is simply looking at an event or situation in a different way. His supposition is clearly illustrated as you review the information shown below. Although humour tends to lose its edge when you analyse it, there are a range of tools that you can use to create humour, including plays on words, understatement, exaggeration, funny stories, presenting an unexpected way of looking at something or playing to the audience's sense of the ridiculous.

Tool 1: The pun or word play

In describing the various forms of humour, *The New Encyclopedia Britannica* refers to a pun as 'two disparate strings of thought tied together by an acoustic knot'. That analogy strikes a very pleasant cord!

Here are a couple of examples to show how puns can give your speech the kiss of life.

Did you hear the story about the man who fell into the upholstery machine but is now fully recovered?

A group of serious chess enthusiasts checked into a hotel and were standing in the lobby discussing their various victories. An hour passed with them still happily talking when the hotel manager came out and asked them to move on. 'But why?' said one of the group and the manager replied: 'I can't stand chess nuts boasting in an open foyer'.

WITH GRATITUDE TO THE ANONYMOUS JOKE WRITERS FOUND ON THE INTERNET

Tool 2: The understatement

An understatement is when a concept or situation is represented less strongly than would be expected. When used to create humour it should be bordering on gross understatement, something that is absurd, preposterous or bizarre.

Talking about an amputated limb: 'Just a flesh wound.'

THE BLACK KNIGHT, *Monty Python and the Holy Grail*

It isn't very serious, I have this tiny little tumour on the brain.

J.D. SALINGER, *The Catcher in the Rye*

Tool 3: The hyperbole

Hyperbole, a gross exaggeration, is the reverse of the understatement. It should be over-the-top, preposterous exaggeration. It is very useful for one-liner quips.

He has the IQ of a wet bathmat.

My husband, Bill, is so thick he thinks postnatal depression is someone having a bad reaction to glue sniffing from postage stamps.

Tool 4: Tell funny stories

Funny stories are really anecdotes, stretched and fleshed to meet your needs. They can be truly yours or you can use poetic licence. Not all of us are able to tell a joke well, but a story is different, especially if it can relate to us. Audiences prefer their humour to be self-deprecating rather than making someone else the butt of the joke.

Humorous stories come from the absurdity of real-life situations. For example, when I had my children, the hospital insisted on giving mothers an enema before the birth. With the birth of my first child, I was feeling very confident – I had done my homework, I knew how to breathe and the labour (at that stage) was perfectly manageable. You could say I was a little cocky.

When they said it was time for the enema I was cooperative but inquisitive about the process. 'Simple,' the nurses said. 'We put this rubber hose into the rectum and pour warm soapy water in and when you feel you cannot take any more water you let us know and you can toddle to the bathroom.'

'Well, that's easy,' I thought, lying on my side, importantly practising my breathing. The nurses busied themselves around me and for what seemed an eternity I could hear the clanking of metal jugs and water sloshing. I was getting fuller and fuller by the minute. I held on, after all I didn't want to appear a wuss. After a decent interval, I calmly indicated that enough was more than enough and that I needed to race rather than toddle to the bathroom.

To which the nurses replied, 'We haven't even started yet'.

Yes, thank your lucky stitches, but that's the stuff of life that makes for a funny story.

Tool 5: A new way of looking at it

Sometimes you might invent a completely different view to the traditional or socially accepted view of a situation or subject in order to create humour.

For example, reverse the generally held belief that 'to queue is desirable, so that each person in turn, is enabled to receive good service'. Take the contrary view that queuing is totally undesirable because it does not allow for self-expression, anarchy, ballroom dancing, shoplifting, violence, and so on. The more outrageous your arguments, the more the audience's sense of the ridiculous will kick in.

Or use celebrities, politicians or key people in the organisation that you are addressing to bring a different perspective to a premise. This would require you to gently caricature the celebrity's lifestyle or thinking. For example, what advice would Elizabeth Taylor, Posh Spice, or Homer J. Simpson give to a new bride?

Tool 6: A sense of the ridiculous

Everyday life situations and events lend you great opportunities for ridicule. Taking life too seriously, as we sometimes do, opens up a Pandora's box of silly moments.

I am watching the arrival in Sydney of the Olympic flame, burning brightly in its miner's lamp, and flown in from Greece on the specially chartered Boeing 747 named Zeus. The sacred flame is here to herald the countdown to the 2004 Olympics. The Deputy Prime Minister and other dignitaries have officially welcomed the flame at the airport. The flame was then whisked away in a cavalcade of security cars to the Sydney Opera House.

The major television channels are broadcasting live, as excitement grows in anticipation of the flame's arrival. When it arrives in less than twenty minutes from the airport in peak-hour traffic (a joke in itself) it is taken to the bowels of the Opera House, presumably to recover from the shock of the dash from the airport. After an inordinately long time it reappears, accompanied by Aboriginal and Greek dancers.

I want to know what it was doing down there, presumably in the Green Room – adjusting its wick? Shedding some light on Olympic security issues? Having a coffee?

The broadcasters use a reverent David Attenborough 'wildlife' whisper in their commentary: 'It will be with us any minute now, I can see movement back there and if we are very still and quiet the flame will appear.'

It's a flame for flipping sake. A flipping flame, no more, no less. Does it need all those security guys and all those millions of euros spent getting it here to make sure it isn't snuffed out on the way?

Evidently this is the last time the flame will come to Australia (unless we manage to acquire the Games again). The last time I will be able to run along beside it and say: 'Is that a flame in your torch or are you just pleased to see me?'

Finding humorous opportunities

- Keep a journal. Keep it with you and write down those funny moments that happen to you or that you hear about from others. Humour comes from everyday life. Look at Jerry Seinfeld who uses everyday nothings to come up with his laidback brand of humour.
- Collect jokes from your favourite comedians – as long as you quote the source and it works in the speech, use it. One of my favourite comedians was a fellow named Tommy Cooper who died in 1984. He left a legacy of silly jokes that still have the world giggling.

I went to the doctor and I said, 'Doctor, I feel like I'm a set of curtains.'

The doctor said, 'For heaven's sake man, pull yourself together.'

I'm not quite sure how I would use this in an after-dinner speech unless I was addressing a medical or curtain manufacturers conference dinner. But if you ever do, ...

- Read the authors who inspire after-dinner-style humour, such as the late P. G. Wodehouse, the English comic novelist. His novels, set in the 1920s and 1930s, gently lampooned the British aristocracy of those times. Many of his writings featured Jeeves, 'the perfect gentleman's gentleman', and his master, Bertie Wooster. Wodehouse's work is still funny today and sets the benchmark for a gentle type of humour that works well in an after-dinner speech.

He was a tubby little chap, who looked as if he had been poured into his clothes and had forgotten to say 'when!'.

The fascination of shooting as a sport depends almost wholly on whether you are at the right or wrong end of the gun.

P. G. WODEHOUSE

How to put it all together

Approach the creation of the after-dinner speech in exactly the same way you would any other speech. It requires the same diligence in identifying the central theme, collating materials, and crafting the speech.

Set the pace or mood by introducing humour very early in the introduction. That will loosen up your audience and gain their attention, so that they are ready to encourage you every minute of the way. Conclusions should always go full circle and be linked to the opening statements; this works especially well in a humorous speech. It is even better if you can manage to achieve this circularity with a final funny line.

Always avoid smutty material. A little risqué is daring and darling, but ribald, rude and offensive is not acceptable for after-dinner speaking. Be guided by your own common sense here. What might be acceptable at a football club dinner would probably not go down well at another function.

The performance

In his book *Sein Language*, Jerry Seinfeld talks about performing: 'Remember, timing, inflection, attitude. That's comedy.' Rehearsal is the time when you discover the suitable timing or rhythm for your speech. It is when you find the right place to pause, change the tonal variation, change your facial expression and adopt the appropriate posture. The mirror will give you a good idea of how you look but this is one speech I recommend you try out on family or friends beforehand. This will give you an indication of where the laughs come and how long you should pause before moving on. This is always a delicate balance because you do not want to cut the laughter short but on the other hand you want to keep moving to keep the momentum going.

Remember also that a larger audience is very different from presenting to a few close people. The secret is to listen to your audience's reaction and, just as the laughter is beginning to die down, continue with the speech. You can learn a great deal from watching comedians and other experienced humorous speakers. You can have a great line but if you do not understand how important delivery is you won't succeed.

As mentioned earlier, you don't need to be a stand-up, knock 'em dead comedian. Even if your lines are lightweight in the humour stakes you can do exceptionally well if you grasp the essentials of posture, timing, rhythm and pause.

> *You don't need to be a stand-up, knock 'em dead comedian …*
> *you can do exceptionally well if you grasp the essentials of posture, timing, rhythm and pause.*

Practice is the answer – the more you do, the more you understand. The more you understand, the more confident you become. The more confident you become, the greater your success.

You need to really think through your appearance for this role. Get the glad rags out of hock. For men it is easy – a good-quality lounge suit, or black tie if the occasion is formal. For women glamour should rule the night. I like to see colour rather than black. Always check your teeth, hair and clothing before speaking.

I recommend not drinking before you deliver the speech. A drink is not going to quell any performance anxiety; it will just take the edge off your performance. Humorous speeches are interactive and you need to listen for cues from your audience, so you want to be alert and attentive.

A 'roast'-style speech

A roast is a fun or satirical way (depending on your perspective) of celebrating a person's achievements. Like the traditional roast meat meal, a roast can be done to different degrees. It does not have to be too raw; it can be well done and palatable so that the guest of honour can walk away at the end of the function feeling pleasantly 'fool' rather than stuffed!

If you have been invited to speak at a roast for some 'lucky' person, the first question you must ask yourself is how sensitive is the 'roastee'? There are some people who should never be the butt of a roast as they are either too sensitive or have a sense of humour that does not run to laughing at themselves. These people will hate it and spend weeks afterwards licking their wounds. Conversely, if the roastee has a good sense of him- or herself and a great sense of humour, then it is relatively 'open season'. However, a word of caution: even the most well-rounded individuals have their vulnerable spots.

If you have received an invitation to take part you probably know the person quite well. Identify those sore spots that will cause the victim to say 'ouch' and make those characteristics a 'roast-free zone'. Choose the target areas to be lampooned carefully and develop your speech. Check with the other speakers to make sure your material is different to theirs.

Develop this speech in the same way you would the humorous speech but always focusing on the roastee. Ideally it should be witty rather than acerbic, clever rather than caustic, and fun rather than frenzied. Remember, it does not have to be all claws drawn and shades of Joan Rivers, Bob Hope, Ben Elton or Judith Lucy to make it effective.

My children gave me a surprise roast party on a milestone birthday and everyone was given a minute to 'roast' me. It was a very happy evening, in spite of my friends' mockery, and I was given a right of reply, so I retaliated with pleasure. One of my kinder friends wrote a clever spoof which she recited at the event and afterwards gave me a framed copy. Needless to say, although I am no national treasure, I just loved it – well, who wouldn't?

The invitation to roast arrived by post.
Of course I would attend!
How could I not be on the spot
When they grilled my very good friend.
I was quite elated although the card stated
That I'd have a minute – no longer;
How could I toast her, let alone roast her,
Before they clanged the donger?
I knew it would be hellish to be roasted with relish,
And, although I'm not much of a cook,
I thought pumpkin would do, with a potato or two,
And so I consulted a book.
There it was in black and white;
Potatoes and pumpkins were fine
To serve with lamb, or even ham,
Or an old chook past its prime.
But nothing did it say about the way
To do justice to a National Treasure.
Abruptly I end
And say to my friend ...
'Mary, you've given us all great pleasure.'

CELEBRITY TIP

The secret to making people laugh is a wink, a smile, a raised eyebrow. Even a deadpan expression can breathe comedy into the blandest of statements.

TANIA NASH

Humour is different things to different people. Some love a play on words, some prefer the cleverness of a well-thought-out one-liner or being introduced to someone else's sense of the ridiculous. It is not what you say that is so vital, but the way you deliver it. When you decide on the tools to use and you have written your speech the key to the best humour lies in the delivery. 'Timing, inflection, attitude' as Jerry Seinfeld said; these will create the laughter every time.

MEDIA
PRESENTATIONS

All you have to do on television is be yourself,
provided, that is, that you have a self to be.

CLIVE JAMES, *The Observer, 1981*

If you are invited to be interviewed on television or radio, here are some hints to make you feel more confident in those environments. There are also tips and techniques to help you shine as you give a demonstration.

While presenting for the media basically requires you to prepare as you would for any speech, that is to identify your central theme and find appropriate resource material, the major difference lies in that you will not be delivering a speech but giving information in mini-speeches as you answer questions. This means that you must make sure that you have a comprehensive knowledge of your topic and have thought through all the angles that the broadcaster may raise. If you are demonstrating a product or craft, you must rehearse meticulously to make sure your performance looks seamless to the viewer.

Television appearances

Seeing television bloopers makes you realise that even television stars are fallible. My television experience has included quite a few bloopers of my own but fortunately they were not collected by an industrious producer to be shown at a later stage. Five years of presenting weekly cooking demonstrations for a couple of daytime television shows was great fun and gave me valuable experience in television presenting.

The first time I presented I was so scared I could hardly breathe. I think my fear came partly from the fact that the television studio and its workings were such unknown territory. I hope that if you are about to enter a television studio or radio station for the first time the information in this chapter will help to settle your nerves.

What to expect when appearing on TV

I have found that most stations give you adequate directions about how to find the studio and whom you should report to. As you arrive at the station you will be checked by security people at the gate, before being directed to the reception or the studio Green Room. The Green Room is a tradition stemming from early days in the theatre when the actors' meeting room was painted a restful shade of green. Nowadays the colour is indifferent and it is simply a pleasant waiting room where guests assemble before they are called onto the set.

Introduce yourself to your contact who will take care of you from here on. They will be able to tell you whether your interview or presentation is running to time. They will take you to the make-up room and introduce you to the make-up person.

If you are doing a demonstration they will help you to set up outside the studio on a mobile bench.

If you have been asked to appear on a current affairs, magazine-style or news program to comment on an issue or to represent a point of view, whether it is yours or that of an affiliated organisation, your appearance may be 'live' or it may be shot prior to the program where it can be edited to the producer's discretion.

If you are presenting an advertorial-style segment of the kind popular on morning television, this will invariably be recorded. Should you make an absolute mess of your presentation, the producer is there to shout 'cut' and do a retake. But time is an expensive commodity in a television studio, so they really do prefer you to get it right the first time.

A television studio is normally a large cavernous place rigged out with banks of spotlights and filled with cameras, cables, boom mikes and more people than you can imagine. If you are allowed into the studio to watch part of the activities of the program you must be very quiet when they are filming.

Once you are on the set the floor manager will give you your cue. He or she will tell you where to sit or stand and which camera to look at or whether to simply look at the interviewer.

Be prepared for delays, as often the running order will be changed to suit the needs of the occasion and you can become pretty frustrated waiting around. Then suddenly, it is your turn. When you reach that stage you will find that the process is very crisp and orderly. The floor manager or producer will give you instructions and then everything is set to go. The floor manager calls for 'quiet', does a countdown and then gives a visual signal to let you know that they are recording or going to air.

What to wear
The camera does tend to stack on extra kilos so wear clothing that slims you down. Most television appearances are from the

waist up so generally this is the area you should concentrate on. Wear a shirt, top or dress that you know suits you and complements your skin colouring. Avoid plain white, as it tends to flare on camera. Off-white or cream-coloured shirts are fine. You can wear black but clear bright colours also look effective.

How to prepare for a television appearance

For an interview you will need to discuss with the producer of the show the questions that they will ask you. If your subject matter is topical or controversial, make sure that you are absolutely *au fait* with what you wish to convey. I would love to be able to tell you that you can trust that every producer or interviewer has your best interests at heart, but that would be naïve. Their job is to make newsworthy television, to ask difficult questions, to lay both sides of a debate bare. You can be sure they will have researched all resources and material and if there is a controversial angle that will make for more dynamic viewing, they will use it.

So be aware, do your own research, and when you have all your material firmly and articulately in place, ask someone you trust to play devil's advocate. Rehearse questions with them and ask them to dream up a few hypothetical curly ones so that you feel confident in your answers. If you are not sure of your facts or are conscious that your opinions may be hung out to dry, don't agree to go on the program. Remember, you do have a choice. Never agree to appear on television unless you are 100 per cent confident in your beliefs or in what you represent.

If you are being interviewed to promote something that you have done or created, the process will be less unpredictable. You can expect questions about your achievements and no doubt the odd personal question.

A demonstration in front of the camera, whether it is cooking, craft or DIY, needs to be thoroughly thought out beforehand. If you are going to appear on a lifestyle show there may well be a team of professionals who will work with you and help prepare all the steps for you. Often, however, you will find that you need to do your own preparation, as well as do all the other necessary things such as visit make-up and liaise with studio staff about other needs such as power or water.

Preparation checklist for a TV demonstration

- Check the amount of time you have to present.

  This is vital knowledge as you will have to condense key actions into this time span and identify beforehand where you need to have a step in the process completed.

- Make enquiries from the studio: will you be alone on camera or will an emcee work with you?

  Normally television stations use an experienced emcee or show host to appear with guests. This means your timing for any activity has to be spot on as you will be talking to someone who may not be overly sensitive to your agenda. You do have the opportunity to talk it through very quickly with them beforehand. This helps but is no guarantee that they will not ask you a question unrelated to your task during the recording.

- Establish your contact at the studio.

  Ask questions such as: do they have a team of people to assist you or will this team have it all set up for you beforehand? If help is not available, you must find out where and how you will present. Where do you find a power source for any equipment you need to use? Is there is a kitchen or separate area where you can do some preliminary preparations? Confirm that the studio will do your make-up. What time do you need to be there? Where can you park and is parking far from the studio? Can they organise a copy of the recording for you?

- Plan out your preparation needs and organise the equipment that you will need to take with you. Think this aspect through very carefully – if the product you are making needs to be broken down into steps, you will need to have an example of each of these steps.

- List your equipment and other needs.
- Prepare a clear and detailed running sheet for use at the studio. This will help you focus and reduce any anxiety.
- Rehearse the stages until your performance runs smoothly and you feel confident with what you are going to say.
- Plan your strategies to manage nerves on the day.
- Assemble everything to take, pack it carefully – think about how you are going to transport it from the car park to the studio.

Radio interviews

An interview on radio is a lot easier than television and takes less of your time. If you have been invited into the station for an interview you can expect to be met at reception and taken to the studio at the appropriate time. When it is time to enter the studio, you will be quickly introduced to the host in between music or ads. You will be given a set of headphones and a microphone will be placed in front of you. The host introduces you and you are into the interview.

You can also do a radio interview via the phone line. The line needs to be stable, that is, a good landline rather than a mobile. However, if there is no alternative, a mobile phone interview will be done. This will be discussed with you when the interview is set up initially. When it is time for your interview they will call you with some time to spare. As you wait, they will keep you abreast of what is happening and you will be able to hear the program going to air through your phone handset. Just before your interview starts, the producer will normally say 'stand by', you hear the introduction and the interview is up and away.

The same rules apply here as for television interviews. Do an interview with your eyes wide open. Remember, the radio host's job is to make interesting listening and they will quiz you. Make sure you know your subject very well. Don't be seduced into speaking on a subject you are not totally committed to or in which you do not have a degree of expertise.

Identify the key points you want to convey to the listening audience. Do your own research on the radio host and the style of questioning that he or she favours. Ask a friend to interview you and to include some tricky questions so that you can practise your answers. Remember to ask for a copy of the tape for your reference and files.

CELEBRITY TIP

One of the key elements is to remember that not all interviewers will do research. Sadly, too many interviewers are badly prepared, don't care or don't know. Help them. Send them information before the interview – websites, examples of your work, good areas for them to explore. Be their researcher and you won't get any surprises.

Prepare yourself as well. Make sure you know what you want to say, and have a clear idea of how to say it. There's nothing wrong with having a few pre-thought-out entertaining, interesting or poignant anecdotes so that if the interview is going off the rails, you can bring it back to an area you feel comfortable with. How many times have you heard great talent say 'It's funny you should ask that, because only the other day ...'? They're doing that to wangle their way out of a dumb, intrusive or difficult question.

Most importantly though, be conversational and interesting. If you're someone that gets nervous, find a good way to relax; if you're known as a chatterbox, learn some verbal discipline. If you aren't interested in what you're talking about, no one else will be either.

SIMON MARNIE

Stage show demonstrations

Demonstrating and speaking is demanding. Not everyone can do it well. It requires you to chat smoothly as you are doing some other activity with your hands. Consider your talents objectively. If you are a focused individual who is uncomfortable doing two things at once, then accept that this role will make you very stressed. You may decide to pass on this opportunity. Demonstrating is taxing, even for the most proficient performer.

Opportunities for stage show demonstrations can vary from a trade show through to a performance at a shopping centre. Each situation will be different. Some venues may have good facilities but others will be abysmal. Virtually all demonstration stages will be temporary or demountable, so they will not provide you with the type of facilities you might enjoy at work.

Ask for that all-important brief and ask the organiser to give you a good understanding of what facilities are available. This advice is relevant whether you are doing a building, gardening, hair and make-up demonstration, handicrafts or food show. Each activity will have its specific needs. Identify the facilities you need and make sure that these demands can be accommodated or that you can be flexible enough to compromise in some fashion. Personal grooming demonstrations or food presentations will be governed by state or local council health regulations and any compromises you may make should not conflict with these. Any conditions need to be sanitary and to have running hot water.

Preparation checklist for a stage show demonstration

- Investigate the facilities, assistance and time you have been allocated to present on stage.
- Enquire about parking and access to the venue.
- Ask if you will be introduced by an emcee.

- What kind of audiovisual equipment will there be? Request a headset or Madonna mike.
- Plan out your demonstration and identify what needs to be done ahead of time.
- Rehearse your demonstration.
- Prepare a list of equipment needed.
- Assemble the equipment and anything else you need.
- Plan to arrive at least an hour early, if not more, especially if you have to fight through crowds to reach the stage area.

Tips for presenting demonstrations

- Prepare a list of adjectives and other helpful words or phrases that will be useful in your demonstration. This is a great strategy for demonstrations, as you always tend to fall back on well-worn vocabulary or favourite lines when you are demonstrating.
- If you have to introduce yourself, include some background information about yourself for the audience. They need to understand that you are qualified to be on the stage giving them the right information.
- Make sure that you have thoroughly rehearsed the techniques involved in your demonstration and that you can continue with your patter as you are doing another activity.
- As you rehearse you might find there will be a repetitious transition word or phrase that you use as you try to move from one part of the demonstration to the next. Or you might not notice it. Ask a friend to watch a rehearsal to pick up on any repetitive words. This is the time to rid your self of poor habits.

  For example, 'okay' is frequently used as link between stages in an activity. Used too often to mark the end of one phase before the speaker moves on to the next phase, 'okay' becomes predictable and slightly irritating to the audience or viewer. Anything that interferes with the intrinsic message is not good.

- Learn to work tightly so you do not mislay any equipment or tools that you may use frequently during the demonstration. You sound and look disorganised if you are continually calling for or trying to find the right tool or piece of equipment.

- Do not take your eyes off any sharp instruments while you are demonstrating. Showmanship is a wonderful thing but badly cutting yourself will unfortunately be the lasting impression your audience will have of your demonstration.

- If your session is being sponsored by a company or association, make sure that you use their correct title and that you represent their products in the manner that they have asked. Read the brief, understand the brief.

- If there is an overhead camera or mirror, make sure you check this out beforehand so that you know where to place things to maximise the viewing opportunity for the audience.

- Be early; be prepared for all eventualities.

- It is important to remember that you are 'on stage' (whatever the venue affords) and it must be a show. Give your presentation all the razzle-dazzle you can muster. Let your enthusiasm shine through.

Television, radio and stage work can be very demanding the first time you do it and you need to be confident in your ability to handle the pressures involved. Self-assurance comes from making yourself an expert on your topic, second guessing all possible questions that you might be asked and, if you are demonstrating, knowing the techniques required like second nature. Above all else, remember to be yourself.

HOW TO CHAIR
A MEETING

Meetings ... are a bit like cocktail parties. You don't want to go but you're cross not be asked.

JILLY COOPER, *How to Survive from Nine to Five*

Understand the responsibilities of chairing a meeting and valuable knowledge about the mechanics of meeting procedures.

In this chapter you can find the basic information needed to chair a meeting. However, by the very nature of the responsibilities of a chairperson (hereafter called the Chair), questions or situations will arise where you will need more in-depth guidance. *Guide for Meetings and Organisations*, by N.E. Renton, is an excellent guide to meeting procedures. Nick Renton is Australia's leading authority on all matters pertaining to meetings. This particular book has been continuously in print for forty years and is a compulsory resource for anyone who has to regularly chair meetings of organisations or associations. The book also has an associated question and answers web page which is extremely useful: <http://users. bigpond.net.au/renton/gmo7.htm>.

The role of the Chair

Some people are confused about the responsibilities of a Chair. The role is more that of a facilitator than an autocrat. This is important to understand as it is not *your* meeting; it is the *members'* meeting and, as Chair, you are there to make sure that the meeting is run in an impartial manner. To be an effective Chair you need to adopt the same nurturing, caring skills as an emcee. Your task is to encourage free and open speech and where necessary to encourage the quieter members of the meeting to have their say. The position requires you to be strong enough to stop an undisciplined debate that is going nowhere.

The act of chairing a meeting is demanding. Your guiding principle should always be what is best for the organisation. This means being prepared at all times and accepting that there will be times when you are not always popular. You need to strive to be consistently fair and remain objective in your management of all matters. As you establish yourself as a reliable, impartial and responsible Chair, you will gain respect from your fellow members and this will flow through in the efficient and smooth running of meetings.

Duties of the Chair

- The primary duty of a Chair, whether you are known as the president of the organisation or by some other title, is to act as Chair at all meetings and in all official activities.
- The Chair must make sure that the organisation, association or club functions smoothly and successfully achieves its objectives.

- You must be conscientious and respectful of the Constitution of the organisation. This means that you must have a thorough knowledge and understanding of your association's Constitution and its intent.

  For those new to the role of committees, the Constitution is a document setting out the aims of the organisation, together with details of the administration set up to achieve these aims. The Constitution may also be known as articles, articles of memorandum, by-laws, charter, regulations, rules or statutes.

- As Chair it is your responsibility to make sure that all meetings are properly convened. You must:
  - Ensure an effective agenda is prepared.
  - Check that all entitled people receive a notice of the meeting and that this complies with the constitutional rules.
  - Check the minutes of the previous meeting to ensure that they have been recorded, to your understanding, correctly.
  - Read any correspondence or reports that have arrived in between meetings so that you are familiar with them before the meeting.

- As Chair you must act in a fair and unbiased way to allow members to have their say. Equally, you must be firm, otherwise the meeting can get out of hand. Always be courteous and tactful and let common sense be your guide.

Meeting procedures

- As Chair you will welcome members to the meeting (giving the meeting its formal title). Be mindful of any protocol such as welcoming visiting VIPs before you welcome your fellow members.
- If there are any alterations to the agenda, announce these at this stage of the meeting. If there are too many, slow your pace so that members can alter their agendas.

- Establish that the meeting has a quorum, the minimum number (as specified by your Constitution) of members present to conduct business.
- If the organisation has a gavel this is the time to use it – at the beginning of the meeting. A gavel is a symbol of authority and traditionally is used to 'call the meeting to order'. The only other time you would use it would be if the meeting became unruly.

The agenda or order of business

In this section we look at the normal order of business or a typical agenda, which is pretty standard for the running order of most meetings. This format will give you the information to easily keep you in control of the meeting. Any order or formality of business will, however, depend on the conventions of your own organisation, so you must defer to these customs where necessary.

While I have included the 'proper' wording for motions in the agenda items, you will need to read the correct procedures for the proposing, seconding and resolution of a motion (see pp. 260–263), which will give you more detailed information on this.

Apologies

In order for the apologies to be accepted and documented in the minutes you will need to establish whether any have come in. First you need to ask the secretary of the organisation 'Are there any apologies?' Prior to the meeting the secretary may have received apologies from members and these names need to be read out. You will then need to ascertain whether other members have apologies to pass on to the meeting: 'Are there are any further apologies from the floor?' If the custom of your organisation is to formally accept the apologies for inclusion in the minutes, then you ask for a motion 'That the apologies be accepted'.

Minutes of the previous meeting

Ask the secretary to read the minutes to the meeting. Some associations may prefer to circulate the minutes prior to the meeting. Either way, you should ask the members 'Is there any discussion regarding the accuracy of the minutes?' Changes should be made if the phrasing or wording misrepresents the meeting's intentions, rather than if they are merely minor grammatical changes. Once these changes have been made, ask again for a proposer to move the motion 'That the minutes as corrected be confirmed'. If there are no corrections to the minutes the motion would be 'That the minutes as read/ circulated be confirmed'. Once the motion has been resolved or passed, initial any changes to the accuracy of the minutes and sign and date the copy of the minutes. Once the minutes have been confirmed they are the *prima facie* (meaning sufficient in law to establish a case or fact, unless disproved) evidence of the proceedings as recorded.

Business arising from the minutes

This is where the preparation of the agenda is important and will keep you on track for a smooth meeting. Simply go through the matters of business that arise from the minutes of the previous meeting. Where action has been called for, make sure that this is reported on by the people responsible for the task. If further action is needed, make sure it is minuted that a report is to be given at the next meeting on the outcome of the task. If motions are needed to achieve the meeting's purpose, ask for appropriate ones to be proposed.

Correspondence

Ask the secretary to list the communications that have come in to the meeting and any that have been sent out. Then ask for a motion that the 'Inwards communications be received'. Once this has been seconded and passed, ask the secretary to read out specific and pertinent correspondence. Routine correspondence need not be read unless it is requested. If there is any business arising from the correspondence, direct that appropriate motions be proposed to facilitate any action the meeting wants to make.

Reports

The President's Report is given annually, while a Treasurer's Report, comprising a brief financial statement, should be given at each meeting. At the Annual General Meeting a balance sheet and annual statement of expenditure should be presented. The wording for the motion to accept these reports (or for most other reports) is 'That this report be adopted'.

It is perfectly acceptable and sometimes desirable to 'receive' some other reports. These are the more minor reports concerning planning of functions or investigating the feasibility of some project. 'Receiving' rather than 'adopting' a report gives the meeting more flexibility to make minor changes at a later date without having to rescind the whole report.

It may be there are some accounts to be paid and so a motion should be stated as 'The accounts as presented be passed for payment'. Any other reports are given following the Treasurer's Report.

Motions on notice

A motion on notice is simply what it says. The reason for a member proposing this style of motion may be to allow people time to consider their proposal or simply a case of running out of time to debate an item that a member wants the meeting to consider. The proposer may move that the subject be adjourned until the next meeting. The Chair must take note of how the debate has progressed and allow a balanced and fair discussion to ensue before asking for the 'motion to be put'.

The intention of this 'motion on notice' is announced at the end of the meeting so that all members are aware of it. This ensures that it will be placed on the agenda for the next meeting.

General business

General business, also known as 'Any other business', is called for at this stage of the meeting. This allows any additional matters that have not already been covered to be raised. These matters may only be discussed if a formal motion is proposed. This is also the proper time for members to present short announcements about other activities.

Dates of the next meeting and conclusion

The Chair calls for the date of the next meeting to be set and the meeting concludes. The Chair should thank everyone for their contributions to the meeting, remind them of the date of the next meeting, and wish them a safe journey.

Correct procedures for the passing, seconding and resolution of motions

Motions

A motion is a proposed instruction, directive or concept that is put forward by a member of the organisation. It needs a seconder to open the discussion before ultimately the debate concludes and the meeting decides the fate of the motion.

There are two kinds of motions – procedural and substantive. A procedural motion takes precedence over a substantive motion.

While you should not become too bogged down in comparing these two types of motions, it is important to have a basic understanding of procedures in case you meet an over-zealous, parliamentary-procedure type who takes great delight in scoring points! The procedural motion deals with the administration and effective running of the meeting. For example, when a debate is going round in circles and it is clear that the matter needs to be put to the vote, the motion from a member would be 'That the motion/question be now put'. Or it might be that the debate is going longer than anticipated and time is running out. However, members want to discuss it further before reaching any conclusions and do not want the motion rushed through without full consideration. The motion for this may be 'That the meeting be adjourned'.

A substantive motion is one that authorises or directs an action or one that expresses the organisation's opinions. For example, 'That the secretary send a letter of protest to the landlord regarding the increase in rent', or 'That this meeting express its strong disappointment in the government's decision to close —— School', or 'That the meeting fees be increased to $10 per week'.

However, for most organisations, business is conducted fairly simply and most members do not distinguish between procedural and substantive motions. If your organisation's practice is more formal and you have any doubts about any procedure, refer to Nick Renton's guide.

Wording of a motion

A motion should always start with 'that'. The motion should be specific and clearly express the intention. An effective motion gets to the nub of the matter succinctly and with clarity. If you, as the Chair, feel that the proposed motion is ambiguous or fuzzy, you should not accept it. You can ask the proposer to reword the motion or you can assist them in rewording it.

Role of the seconder

The purpose of having someone second a motion is to establish that there is support for the proposal and to open up discussion of the motion. The seconder can speak to the subject there and then or defer their right to speak until later in the debate. The seconder does not necessarily have to be in favour of the motion. They may simply want to open it up to allow free and open discussion of the subject.

Rules for debating a motion

Once a motion has been seconded the Chair asks for someone to speak against the motion and subsequently for alternative speakers to speak for and against the motion. The proposer of the motion has the right to speak a second time. Once the proposer speaks for a second time the debate is closed automatically and the vote takes place.

Some smaller meetings prefer a more relaxed approach to the rules of debate and allow members to speak more than once. Whatever the customs of your organisation, matters must be recorded in the minutes and as Chair you must make sure that the debate is carried out in an orderly and civilised manner.

For the sake of efficient and energy-saving meetings do not let the debate go on too long before the motion is put or you may find a member doing this for you by proposing a motion 'That the motion/question be now put'. Because it is a procedural motion you would have to deal with this motion first. It would then need a seconder and if it were passed you would then put the other (substantive) motion to the vote.

Passing a motion

As Chair you should now read the motion and ask members to vote on it. Voting can be by a show of hands, a secret vote that members record on an appropriate form, or by asking 'All those in favour please say aye'. It might be that someone feels strongly and wishes to have his or her dissension recorded in the minutes; if so, that should be done.

Election of any new members

The election of members to positions as office bearers must always be carried out strictly in accordance with the rules and regulations of your organisation's Constitution.

It might be preferable for you to vacate the Chair during this process, especially if you are involved in the election procedures. You will need to organise a replacement Chair for these proceedings.

It is the Chair's responsibility:

- to verify the credentials of those nominated
- if your Constitution allows, to call for nominations from the floor and to declare the nominations closed
- if you have the right number of candidates for the number of vacancies, to declare all those candidates duly elected
- if you have more candidates than vacancies, to announce the election and give clear instructions to members how this will be conducted. An officer of the organisation should oversee the election procedure
- to announce the results of the election and to declare these people duly elected.

The key point to remember when chairing a meeting is that you are in control of the logistics (not necessarily of the outcome) of the meeting procedures. Your job is to make sure that everyone has an equal opportunity to speak if they wish to and that the rules and best interests of the organisation are adhered to. People will long remember you as Chair if you exercise impartiality and good judgement rather than a detailed knowledge of correct procedures and protocol.

FURTHER
READING

Adams, A.K., *Cassell's Book of Humorous Quotations*, Cassell,
     London, 1969.

Agel, Jerome, & Glanze, Walter D., *Pearls of Wisdom: A Harvest of
     Quotations from All Ages*, Harper & Row, New York, 1987.

Armstrong, David F., Stokoe, William C., & Wilcox, Sherman E.,
     Gesture and the Nature of Language, Cambridge University
     Press, New York, 1995.

Brandreth, Giles, *Everyman's Modern Phrase and Fable*, J.M. Dent,
     London, 1990.

Browning, D.C., *Treasury of World Masterpieces: Dictionary of
     Quotations and Proverbs – The Everyman Edition*, Octopus
     Books, London, 1982.

Bryson, Bill, *Mother Tongue*, Penguin, Harmondsworth, UK, 1991.

Buzan, Tony & Barry, *Mind Map Book: How to Use Radiant
     Thinking to Maximise Your Brain's Untapped Potential*, E.P.
     Dutton, New York, 1994.

Cohen, J.M., & M.J., *The Penguin Dictionary of Quotations*,
     Penguin, Harmondsworth, UK, 1980.

Crystal, David, & Crystal, Hilary, *Words on Words*, Penguin, London, 2000.

De Bono, Edward, *Six Thinking Hats*, International Center for Creative Thinking, New York, 1985.

Ely, Virginia, *I Quote*, Lutterworth Press, London, 1964.

Evans, Bergen, *Dictionary of Quotations*, Avenel Books, New York, 1978.

Fitzhenry, Robert I., *The David & Charles Book of Quotations*, David & Charles, Newton Abbot, London, 1986.

Flavell, Linda, & Roger, *Dictionary of Idioms and their Origins*, Kyle Cathie, London, 1997.

Fuller, Edmund, *2500 Anecdotes for All Occasions*, Avenel Books, New York, 1978.

Greenfield, Susan A., *The Human Brain: A Guided Tour*, Weideneld & Nicolson, London, 1997.

Harris, Carol, *NLP Made Easy*, Element, London, 2003.

Henry, Lewis C., *Best Quotations for All Occasions*, Ballantine Books, New York, 1991.

How to Write and Speak Better, Reader's Digest (Australia), Sydney, 1989.

Kennedy, Kevin, *A Pageant of Words*, Doubleday, Moorebank, NSW, 1988.

Kingsolver, Barbara, *The Poisonwood Bible,* Faber & Faber Ltd, London, 2000.

Kubler-Ross, Elisabeth, *On Death and Dying*, Simon & Schuster, New York, 1997.

Manser, Martin, *Dictionary of Word and Phrase Origins*, Sphere Books, London, 1990.

McDermott, Ian, & Jago, Wendy, *The NLP Coach*, Judy Piatkus, London, 2001.

Metcalf, Fred, *The Penguin Dictionary of Modern Humorous Quotations*, Penguin, Ringwood, Victoria, 1986.

Peale, Norman Vincent, *The Power of Positive Thinking*, Prentice Hall, New York, 1952.

Pease, Allan, *Signals: How to Use Body Language for Power, Success and Love*, Bantam Books, Sydney, 1984.

Pease, Allan & Pease, Barbara, *Definitive Guide to Body Language*, HarperCollins, Australia, 2004.

Pepper, Frank. S., *Handbook of 20th Century Quotations*, Sphere Books, London, 1984.

Perls, Frederick, S., *In and Out the Garbage Pail*, Bantam Books, New York, 1972.

Powers, John, *Winning*, Sphere Books, Melbourne, 1982.

Rees, Nigel, *Cassell Dictionary of Clichés*, Cassell, London, 1996.

Renton, N.E., *Guide for Meetings*, The Law Book Company, North Ryde, NSW, 1990.

Renton, N.E., *Guide for Voluntary Associations*, The Law Book Company, North Ryde, NSW, 1991.

The Right Word at the Right Time, Reader's Digest Association, London, 1985.

Samuel, Viscount, *A Book of Quotations*, The Cresset Press, London, 1945.

Schwartz, David J., *The Magic of Thinking Big*, Simon & Schuster, New York, 1987.

Seinfeld, Jerry, *Sein Language*, Bantam Books, New York, 1998.

Shreve, Anita, *The Pilot's Wife*, Little, Brown & Co., London, 1999.

Sumner, Peter, *I Like That*, The Christian Foundation for the Blind, Hawthorn, Vic., 1979.

INDEX

267